W9-BLA-414

GENESIS

by

HOWARD F. VOS

MOODY PRESS
CHICAGO

CONTENTS

© 1982 by
THE MOODY BIBLE INSTITUTE
OF CHICAGO

The use of selected references from various versions of the
Bible in this publication does not necessarily imply publisher
endorsement of the versions in their entirety.

Library of Congress Cataloging in Publication Data

Vos, Howard Frederic, 1925-
  Genesis.
  Bibliography: p. 174.
  1. Bible. O.T. Genesis—Commentaries. I. Title.
BS1235.3.V67   222'.1107   81-18770
ISBN 0-8024-2001-X   AACR2

2 3 4 5 6 7 Printing/LC/Year 87 86 85 84 83

Printed in the United States of America

1

BACKGROUNDS

Most of us are vitally interested in answers to the big questions of life. Where did we come from? Why are we here? What makes us tick, or what is the nature of man? How did we get into the mess we are in? What is our future? Or what is the future of the world? We consider any literature that deals with those questions relevant and timely.

Preeminent among all literature about the big questions of life is the book of Genesis. Its name comes from a Greek word, *geneseos,* which was the title given it in the Septuagint (Greek translation of the Old Testament). That title was derived from the heading of the various sections of the book, each of which begins with "the book of the geneseos" (meaning *generation, origin, source;* see 2:4; 5:1; 6:9; 10:1; 11:10, 27; 25:12, 19; 36:1, 9; 37:2). In these sections Genesis depicts the beginning of the world by creation; the beginning of mankind and human languages; the beginning of sin in the race; the beginning of salvation; the beginning of God's chosen people, Israel; the beginning of the Arabs (descended from Ishmael, 25:12) and the other nations of the earth; the beginning of the Arab-Israelite conflict; and the beginning of the covenant with Abraham and his descendants. The latter in its fuller statement and with its supplements spells out conditions at the end time—Jews in control of the promised land and their Messiah ruling on the throne of David in Jerusalem.

As a book of beginnings, Genesis is of course a seed plot and springboard for the concepts and history of the rest of the Old Testament. But it is almost nearer in many ways to the New Testament than the rest of the Old Testament. As Derek Kidner has observed, the institution of marriage, the Fall of man, judgment by Flood, Esau's despising his birthright, and many of its other themes are hardly dealt with again until the New Testa-

ment. Moreover, whereas near the beginning of Genesis Satan
is victorious and man is expelled from Eden, in a beautiful sym-
metry the New Testament ends with the serpent coming to his
downfall and the redeemed walking again in Paradise.[1]

Probably over no other part of Scripture have so many battles
been fought as over the book of Genesis. Theologians, scientists,
historians, and students of literature have subjected it to minute
examination and criticism. But with all their attention, they have
been able neither to exhaust its contents nor destroy its message.
The measure of its greatness is seen in its continuing ability to
command the attention of scholars and laymen alike throughout
the world.

AUTHORSHIP

One of the battles fought over Genesis has concerned its authorship. But of course the authorship of Genesis is closely tied to
that of the rest of the Pentateuch (first five books of the Old Testament). Eighteenth-century rationalism launched attacks against
the Pentateuch along with the rest of the Bible. Denying any
supernatural origin of Scripture, it completely humanized the
Bible and viewed it as a record of man's experience with God
rather than a revelation of God to man. And as the teachings of
evolution made an increasing impact during the nineteenth century, the concept of slow development was applied to Scripture.
Thus it was taught that the Pentateuch developed gradually:
documents and sources were collected and edited until it finally
came to its present form during the fifth century B.C. Mosaic
authorship was denied.

Theories of literary development not employed in dealing with
other literature were forced on the Scripture in a day when Near
Eastern studies had not yet provided a basis for evaluating theories of biblical interpretation. In fact, construction of liberal
theories did not even make common-sense allowance for vari-
ations in style and vocabulary with differences in subject matter
and mood of the author, and highly subjective conclusions were
reached.

Discussion of that highly technical subject is beyond the scope
of this study. It is enough for present purposes to show that
there is abundant support for the traditional view of Mosaic

authorship. The Pentateuch itself claims that important parts were written by Moses (e.g., Ex. 24:4, 7; Deut. 31:9, 24-26). Internal evidence shows that the Pentateuch was written by an eyewitness. Those parts that involve Egypt contain many references that show the author's familiarity with Egypt and have information virtually impossible to obtain in Canaan several centuries after Moses' day, when liberals hold it was written. Egyptian names, Egyptian words borrowed by the writer, Egyptian customs and geography all indicate the author knew Egypt well.

Pentateuchal claims for Mosaic authorship are supported in the rest of the Old Testament, intertestamental literature, and the statements of Christ. As early as Joshua's day the law of Moses was in written form (Josh. 1:7-8; 8:32, 34; 22:5). And the rest of the Old Testament follows Joshua's example (e.g., 1 Kings 2:3; 2 Chron. 23:18; 34:14; Ezra 3:2; 6:18; Neh. 8:1-8; Dan. 9:11, 13).

The testimony continues during the intertestamental period, notably in Ecclesiasticus 45:6 (written about 180 B.C.) and in Philo (*Life of Moses* 3:39), dating about the time of Christ's birth. Those are supported by the eminent Josephus (*Antiquities* IV.8.48), who wrote about A.D. 90. All three declare Mosaic authorship of the Pentateuch.

Christ on numerous occasions spoke of the law of Moses, sometimes of the "book of Moses" (Mark 12:26), and twice of "Moses and the prophets" (Luke 16:29, 31) or Moses, the prophets, and the psalms (Luke 24:44), obviously making Moses author of the first part of the Old Testament on a par with the other major sections. The early church, the church of later centuries, and the Jews almost unanimously accepted that view until the rise of destructive higher criticism at the end of the nineteenth century. The position is too strongly supported to be dismissed easily by a group of rationalists.

Of course the claim that Moses wrote the Pentateuch in general or Genesis in particular does not assume that Moses wrote without the use of sources. Inspiration argues only for accuracy of the written record; it does not stipulate that the writer had a mind that functioned as a blank tablet to be written on by the Holy Spirit. Abraham came from a very sophisticated background in which all sorts of records were meticulously kept. Joseph rose to a place of leadership in a very literate society; if he himself did not write, he had plenty of scribes who did. Both of these men could have contributed to the written sources available to Moses; and of course many could have contributed oral sources.

Interesting confirmation of the traditional view of single authorship of Genesis has been provided by a five-year linguistic analysis of the book, just completed in Israel. The study was conducted at Technion, Israel's institute of technology in Haifa, under the direction of Professor Yehuda Radday. It reached the conclusion that there was an 82% probability that Genesis was written by one author.[2]

DATE OF COMPOSITION

When Moses wrote Genesis will never be known, but the latest possible date is the time of his death, just before the Hebrews crossed the Jordan and attacked Jericho. The time of that event depends on the date one assigns to the Exodus. This writer subscribes to the early date of the Exodus (about 1440) and thus concludes that Genesis must have been written by about 1400 B.C., for Moses died at the end of the subsequent forty years of wilderness wandering.

CONTENTS AND OUTLINE

The book of Genesis divides rather easily into two parts: the early history of mankind (chaps. 1-11), and the patriarchs (chaps. 12-50). The first part narrates the creation of the universe and mankind and quickly moves on through the story of the entrance of sin into the world, the extension of godless civilization, judgment on humanity by means of the Flood, and further judgment by means of proliferation of languages and scattering across the earth. Then in part two God makes a fresh beginning by calling out a new people as a witness to His name in the earth. That people, the Hebrews, are led by patriarchs (Abraham, Isaac, Jacob) during a 215-year period in Canaan; at the end of the book they go down into Egypt to escape a famine and are cared for there through the instrumentality of Joseph.

OUTLINE

Part 1: THE EARLY HISTORY OF MANKIND (1:1–11:32)
    The Creation (1:1–2:3)
    The Fall of Man and Extension of Civilization (2:4–5:32)
    The Flood (6:1–9:29)
    Historical Developments After the Flood (10:1–11:32)

Part 2: THE PATRIARCHS (12:1–50:26)
    Abraham (12:1–25:18)
    Isaac (25:19–26:35)
    Jacob (27:1–36:43)
    Joseph (37:1–50:26)

NOTES

1. Derek Kidner, *Genesis* (Downers Grove, Ill.: Inter-Varsity, 1967), p. 14.
2. "Computer Points to Single Author for Genesis," *New York Times*, 8 November 1981.

2

THE CREATION

In simple, concise, nontechnical language Moses answers one of the big questions of life: "Where did the earth come from?" Says Moses, "In the beginning God created the heaven and the earth" (KJV).* Then with broad strokes of the pen he proceeds to sketch out six creative days that culminate with a description of the origin of the first human couple, thus answering another of the big questions of life: "Where did man come from?" These verses are truly a masterpiece, suitable for the plain people of his day and all succeeding ages. Yet they do not close the door on scientific and philosophical investigation, for they state only *that* God created, and do not describe how. Nor does Moses say when creation took place. "In the beginning," at the outset of this phase of His creative work, God called into being the heaven and earth; at the end of the process He created man. If God left open the question of the date of origin, we may also.

The Prologue (1:1-2)

"In the beginning God." God is the subject of the first sentence of the book, and He dominates the entire chapter. Called by His name *Elohim* thirty-five times in the creation narrative, He demonstrates infinite power and transcends all material existence, as indeed the majestic name *Elohim* signifies. "Beginning" refers to the commencement of time in our universe and demonstrates that the matter of the universe had a definite origin; it is not eternal and did not start itself. "Created" translates the Hebrew *bārā'*, which Hebrew scholars commonly have understood to signify to bring into being *ex nihilo*, from nothing, without the use of preexisting material. But even some evangelical Old Testament

---

King James Version. Unless otherwise specified, the biblical text used in this commentary is the author's own translation.

scholars do not now believe that the case for such a position is impregnable. If it is not, support for *ex nihilo* creation may be found in the New Testament, as Hebrews 11:3 and Romans 4:17 demonstrate. "Heaven and earth" seems to mean the whole universe, not only planet earth and its enveloping atmosphere.

Some commentators prefer to treat Genesis 1:1 as a dependent clause, and they produce translations such as "When God began to create the heavens and earth, the earth was without form and void." Such a translation implies that the condition of verse 2 already existed when God began to create. E. J. Young argues cogently against such a view and for the position that 1:1 is an independent clause, meant to be a "simple declaration of the fact of absolute creation.[1]

In the past many have conjectured that a great catastrophe occurred between Genesis 1:1 and 1:2. They could not conceive of God's creating a chaos, and therefore supposed that something happened to spoil the original, beautiful, and perfect creation and to necessitate God's recreation in six creative days. Some would place here the fall of Satan and the entrance of sin into the universe to deface what God had made. In setting forth that concept, they were able to introduce a vast time span between original creation and recreation and thus to find a way to bring about some meeting of minds between the claims of scientists about the age of the universe and the beliefs of many Bible students.

In dealing with such a view, it should be noted first that verse 2 only describes the world as "desolate and uninhabitable," at a stage not yet ready for man. It does not portray chaos as such. Presumably God did not determine to bring the creation to a completed state all at once, though He could have done so. Second, there is no direct or specific statement anywhere in Scripture of divine judgment between those verses. Third, there is no justification for translating, "and the earth *became* desolate." The verb normally is rendered "was" throughout the Old Testament; Harold G. Stigers argues that the Hebrew construction does not warrant the translation "became" here.[2]

Darkness enveloped the primeval ocean, but the Spirit of God began to move "upon the face of the waters." God's creative and sustaining energy in the form of the Holy Spirit began to work on the creation in process. Thus the entire Trinity participated in the creation. It would appear that the Father was the designer and issued the decree to create; the Son effected the design (John 1:3; Col. 1:16); and the Spirit was involved in some capacity. Matter apart from God is inert and has no ability to produce a world of order and beauty, but the omnipotent and intelligent Holy Spirit imparts capacity to matter and produces an ordered world.

The Creative Process (1:3—2:3)

Having accounted for the origin of the universe, Moses now concentrates on a geocentric or earth-centered view of creation. What he comments on primarily concerns the development of the earth and making it a proper habitation for humanity. Nothing is said about numerous other creative activities of God (e.g., angels, other solar systems). This process is described as taking place on six creative days.

Length of Creative Days. But immediately a question arises concerning the length of the creative days. Various answers have been given.

1. Literalists down through the millennia have assumed that they were approximately twenty-four hours in length and have supported their conclusions with an appeal to an apparent twenty-four-hour cycle in the passage (day and night, evening and morning). Such references as Exodus 20:11 also have been used to uphold that position. Such views are maintained even though the sun is not mentioned until the fourth day.

2. Especially as a result of geological studies and acceptance of a belief in the great age of the earth, many have espoused a day-age theory: that the days were extended periods of time. It is argued that even in the Genesis narrative "day" may be variously construed: (a) daylight as opposed to night (1:5, 14-16), (b) a solar day of twenty-four hours (1:14), (c) or the entire six-day creative period (2:4).

A position similar to the day-age concept is that held by Davis A. Young. He argues that the sabbath of creation week has not yet ended and therefore is to be viewed as a *figurative* day, a long indeterminate period. He concludes that the seventh day is the key to understanding creation week and that all the other six days also are figurative days. By this he does not mean that the creation narrative is unhistorical but that the days are not literal, consecutive twenty-four hour segments of time.[3] Other scholars have come to a similar conclusion.

3. Literal days with gaps. This theory preserves the creation days as twenty-four hour periods but holds that the days need not be stacked one against the other. Between the creative intervention of God extended periods of time may have elapsed.

4. The Revelatory Day theory, or Days of Dramatic Vision, holds that God over a period of six days revealed His creative work in a series of visions; the account is not a record of what He *performed* in six days. Few have espoused this position. What appears in Genesis 1 is not in the language of vision but historical narration.

Historicity of the Creation Account. Evolutionary and humanistic influences have encouraged a tendency to view the early chapters of Genesis as allegorical and poetic. That approach especially has been taken toward chapter 1. But it should be noted that the poetic parallelism of Hebrew poetry is missing from chapter 1 (except for vv. 26-27), and the rest of the early part of Genesis for that matter. And Genesis 2:4a connects the first verses of the book with the later genealogical orientation and presupposes the contents of chapter 1. As the reader proceeds through the early chapters of Genesis, he does not sense a change of pace or literary structure that would give any hint that he was passing from allegory or poetry or myth to history. Moreover, the New Testament treats the creation as a historical process. Paul taught that God created the world (Acts 17:24) and that man was made in the image of God (1 Cor. 11:7); Hebrews attributed creation to the Word of God (Heb. 11:3).

The Creation Week. The creation narrative is brief and concise. No doubt much more happened on each creative day than is reported in Scripture; evidently in each case only the major categories of activity are reported. Thus, the fact that plant life appeared especially on the third day is no clear-cut evidence that some new forms of plant life did not appear on the fourth or a later day, or that some primitive forms of life such as algae did not appear on the second day. That is an important point to keep in mind when seeking to equate the creative days of Genesis with geologic ages or geologic information. There is remarkable gen-

eral agreement between the two as currently understood. That
agreement may increase with new discoveries and modifications
of geologic scholarship. At least there is no scientific evidence
that proves the general order of creative events in Genesis to be
in error.

The first day (1:3-5). God *spoke* light into existence. What
was that creative word? It involved the action of His will's determining what was to happen and the operation of omniscient
intelligence's shaping objects in the most magnificent possible way,
down to the last atom. On each of the six days God's creative
word generated (1:3, 6, 9, 11, 14, 20, 24, 26). The writer to the
Hebrews referred to that creative utterance when he said: "The
worlds were framed by the word of God" (11:3). And the psalmist in alluding to the creation said, "He spoke, and it was done"
(33:9).

The nature of that light is debated. Some call it a sort of cosmic
light because the sun, moon, and stars are said to have been created on the fourth day. But others observe that the sun could
have been in existence at that time but did not specifically begin
to serve its visible functions in relation to the earth until the
fourth day. Whatever the light, apparently the earth at that time
first received light in order to be a fit place for the inhabitants for
which it was intended.

The second day (1:6-8). As God continued to give form to the
world, He next brought into being a "firmament," something that
according to the Hebrew was spread out, put firmly in place, that
is, the "vault of heaven." That firmament He called *heaven*, not
the abode of God, but the sky, as verses 9 and 20 indicate. Reference is to the gaseous atmosphere.

The formation of the atmosphere was achieved by dividing the
waters under the atmosphere from those above it. Originally the
earth may have been surrounded by a "cloud-fog" condition or a
"watery fluid," which would have made life as we know it virtually impossible. Now the waters under the atmosphere were
separated more distinctly from those above it, and the ocean thus
was formed.

What were the waters above the atmosphere? Apparently they
were ordinary rain clouds. Some have been attracted to the theory that they refer to a water vapor canopy that enveloped the

earth; that was brought into being during the creative process and dissipated at the time of the Noahic Flood. Davis A. Young shows that Scripture itself militates against such a view. For instance, in Psalm 148 when the psalmist calls on creation to praise the Creator God, it commands the "waters that be above" the heavens to praise God (v. 4). Those waters are still above the heavens, and verse 6 indicates they are to stay there "for ever and ever" in response to God's unalterable decree.[4]

The third day (1:9-13). The process of differentiation continued, with the water's being separated from earth so that instead of there being a vast globe-encircling ocean, water was localized in oceans and lakes and rivers, and dry land appeared (probably by means of considerable seismic and volcanic activity). That dry land eventually would then be suitable for plant life, animal life, and human life.

As the dry land appeared, God brought into being a profusion of flora that could reproduce and cross-breed and develop new species—but within limits: "after his kind" (see subsequent discussion on evolution). It should be noted that whenever biological references appear subsequently, those limits are imposed. Any development or mutation that God permits cannot go beyond certain bounds. As the earth began to take on a more distinctive character and was filled with life and beauty, God was pleased with what was produced.

The fact that animal fossils frequently appear older than plant fossils or are contemporary with them does not particularly worry geologist Davis A. Young. As he points out, plant fossils are harder to preserve and harder to find than animal fossils, land plant fossils cannot be expected to appear in marine rocks (and a great many of the fossil-bearing rocks we possess are of marine character), and the evidence at present is very incomplete.[5] Material that has come to light does not prove the Genesis account to be wrong in placing the origin of most plants on the third creative day and most animal life on the fifth day.

The fourth day (1:14-19). The Hebrew text of these verses may not indicate that the sun, moon, and stars came into existence at this time; the word for "create" (*bārā'*) used earlier in the chapter does not occur in verse 16. Possibly God created all the heavenly bodies in the earlier stages of creation (v. 1), and they developed toward their present form as the earth did. Now those light bearers are assigned their relationship to the earth as twin regulators to establish days, seasons, and years. Evidently the present arrangement of the universe operating according to natural law came into being. Alternatively, it is argued that the word used for "made" (*'äsä*) in verse 16 frequently is a synonym of *bärä'* and that God did indeed create those heavenly bodies at that point.

The fifth day (1:20-23). As the creative process continued, the waters of the earth were now ready for marine life and the land and atmosphere prepared for fowl. Food and habitation were available to all. Seaweeds, grasses, trees and other growing things provided for new forms of life. "Let the waters teem" indicates the rapid filling of the waters with marine life, but it may not necessarily mean that there were no lower forms of marine life (e.g., corals, sponges) before that time. If there were, there is no conflict between Scripture and science, which reports existence of fossils of elementary forms of marine life supposedly dating earlier than those of some plants. "Flying things" seems to include insects as well as birds.

"And God created great sea monsters." The use of *bärä'* (create) shows that the origin of those creatures is a result of direct divine action and not merely of some indirect control of a process of natural development. And the appearance of the monsters at this juncture shows that they came from God's good hand and manifest the might of His power. They are not to be viewed as rivals of deity as was true of the sea monsters described in pagan mythology. As the oceans and the earth began to fill up with wildlife, God was pleased with the result (v. 22) as He was on the third day (v. 12). And as on day three, God specifically restricted reproduction ("after his kind"). Whatever cross-breeding or development might occur, divine limits were imposed and presumably a full-scale evolutionary process without divine control ruled out.

The sixth day (1:24-31). On the sixth day land animals and man crowned God's creative work. Having populated the sea and the sky and having blanketed the earth with herbage, He next turned to filling the earth itself with living creatures. In verse 24 three classifications of terrestrial life are listed: cattle (animals capable of domestication), creeping things (reptiles or a variety

of short-legged creatures that may appear to crawl), and beasts of
the earth (truly wild animals that usually cannot be domesticated). All three of these categories, like other creatures previously created, reproduce only after their kind.

As the crowning event of creation week God created man. It is
evident that man is to be so considered because he was given
dominion over all that God had previously created, and man was
created in the image of God Himself. It is interesting to note that
when God spoke of creating man, He used three first person plural
pronouns: "Let *us* make . . . in *our* image, after *our* likeness . . ."
Those indicate plurality in the Godhead, perhaps a full Trinitarian
relationship. And whereas God, unspecified as to person, under-
took to create other details of the universe, here the Godhead together cooperated in the creation of man, giving distinction to the
work in which God was now engaging.

To leave no doubt that man was a special creation, verse 27
three times states that God created man and uses the verb *bārā'*,
indicating a special creation. It is almost as if He anticipated a
later denial of that position by modern naturalists. He made both
male and female (complementary personalities) on the sixth day,
as is clear from verse 27; but the details of the creation of woman
appear in chapter 2.

As a special creation of God, human beings were produced in His
image and likeness. Apparently that likeness to God involved both
a natural and a moral likeness. By nature, man was like God in
that he was a personal being possessing self-consciousness, self-
determination, and knowledge or intellect. Man's moral likeness
consisted of his sinlessness. On the basis of both the moral and
natural likeness, man could have fellowship with God. When man
sinned, he lost the moral likeness, and fellowship with God was
severed. But man still possesses a natural likeness to God, and
therefore deserves the respect of other human beings (Jas. 3:9).
Would it make a difference in human relations if we recognized
that all with whom we come in contact are human beings truly
created in the image of God?

As a consequence of the divine image, man was to exercise dominion over all creatures; and fallen man still largely exercises it
(Jas. 3:7-8). His commission to subdue the earth called forth all
his powers of wisdom and energy. Natural obstacles had to be

overcome. Mineral wealth had to be discovered and processed. Unfortunately, in our sinful state we too often fall into the evil of exploiting the earth, its resources, and its creatures, rather than assuming the responsibilities of stewardship.

Man also was to multiply and "fill" the earth, not "replenish" it, as in the King James Version. There is no basis here for the theory that the earth once had been populated and now needed to be repopulated after some catastrophe (e.g., between vv. 1 and 2). Filling the earth would require adaptation to various climates and geographical conditions.

Finally, God gave "every green plant for food" to man and to the other living beings He had created. It is questionable that this means no animals were carnivorous or that man was to be vegetarian. And it probably does not mean that all plants were edible. The primary point is that God had made provision for all living creatures.

At the end of the creative process God surveyed what He had made and pronounced it "very good." Coming from the hand of God, it could not be otherwise.

The seventh day (2:1-3). Having completed the work of creation, God "rested" or "ceased from work." Then He determined to set aside that seventh day as a special day for Himself. His resting became the basis for the commandment to man to observe the Sabbath (Exodus 20:8-11). "The Sabbath was made for man and not man for the Sabbath" (Mark 2:27-28). God does not need it, for "the Creator of the ends of the earth faints not, neither is weary" (Isa. 40:28). Thus the creation week, whatever its length, became a prototype of a division of time not suggested by nature; rather it is of divine appointment. By contrast, the day, month, and year result from the dictates of nature.

Creation or Evolution. In the foregoing discussion of the creative process, the position has been taken that the Genesis account is factual and historical. The events did occur in the sequence indicated and God was responsible for bringing into being the earth and all that is on it.

That position is of course in direct conflict with the commonly accepted monophyletic evolutionary hypothesis. According to that view, beginning with self-reproducing chemicals and one-celled forms, there was a slow development over a very long period of time through plant and animal stages until man finally appeared on the scene. The process is thought to work by mutation and natural selection. That is to say, living organisms change (mutate) and may pass on those mutations to forms they generate. Those forms best able to adjust to their environment (the "fittest") survive and reproduce; others simply die out. Nature itself determines which are the most fit (natural selection). It is popular to deny that there has been any divine influence on those processes.

At first glance, contemporary scientific theory and the Bible seem to be at direct opposites. And they are as far as basic philosophy is concerned, because the one postulates a purely natural process and the other a development with God's taking the initiative and in supervisory control. But the result of the two positions or the outworking of the process may not be at such great odds.

In trying to effect a reconciliation between the two positions, it is well to observe that Genesis first of all does not say *how* God created but only *that* He did. Nor does it say how long He took to get the job done. As cases in point, the biblical account declares that God separated earth and water and formed the oceans of the world. He could have just spoken and achieved such a result, it is said, or He could have moved through an extended geological process during which mountains were elevated and basins depressed and continents brought into being. He brought into existence plants and animals. He could have created large numbers of species or just a limited number of primordial forms from which the others developed.

An important means of coming to terms with contemporary scholarship concerns itself with the "kinds" of Genesis 1. All of nature is said to reproduce "after its kind" (Hebrew, *min*), not to cross certain divinely fixed boundaries. No one knows exactly what *min* should be equated with in our biological classification—genera? families? or something else? In other words, there seems to be some room here for mutation (or change) and even natural (or supernatural) selection.

For instance, we may observe that there are many varieties of cats or dogs or cows, and those may have descended from one parent "kind" that existed in Eden or on the ark of Noah. Thus, there may have been mutation from the parent dog, and selection to produce the many varieties now known; but dogs always produce dogs—"after their kind." Likewise, the Bible refers to only one human pair, but there are many races and subraces in the world today. Obviously there had to be some changes to produce those anthropological differences, but man cannot crossbreed or hybridize with any animals and can produce only man—"after his kind."

All this adds up to saying that Bible believers may accept a certain amount of variation in nature and, in that way, achieve some degree of a meeting of minds with modern science. But the extent of that change or diversification appears to have fixed limits (within "kinds"), according to Scripture and science. The "missing links" are numerous indeed.

Another way of achieving a meeting of minds with contemporary scholarship is through a form of polyphyletic evolution. The common evolutionary hypothesis follows monophyletic evolution, development from one-celled forms up through plant and animal forms to man. But there is a minority view called polyphyletic evolution. That position holds that there were several phyla, orders or families, proceeding side by side in independent development. If a Bible student were to accept the view, for instance, that God created spermatophyte groups (flowering plants) or mollusk categories (shellfish and octopuses), from which all the individual varieties in those classifications developed; and if a student of natural science were to accept the view that such groups did exist and develop independently side by side, there would be little basic conflict in the process of development taught by each. But of course the moving power in the one case would be supernatural and in the other natural.

It should be stressed, however, that at present polyphyletic evolution is held by few. The common position is monophyletic evolution. In dealing with that form of evolution, several observations are in order.

1. Such evidence as natural scientists have marshaled for evolution has been for micromutation rather than macromutation, for minor departures from parent types rather than major ones that might cross family or genus lines. There is no evidence for the crossing over from plant to animal life or for moving from one type to another except in a microevolutionary sense. To put the matter in another way, there is lack of sufficient intermediate forms

("missing links"), and scientists are unable to prove genetic continuity among various organisms living and extinct. Some might consider hybrids to be an exception, but they occur only between similar members of the same group.

2. Whereas the evolutionary hypothesis builds on movement from simple to complex in an upward curve, all mutations are detrimental except within a narrow range of environmental conditions.

3. The hypothesis does not satisfactorily explain the origin of simple life in the universe but usually assumes spontaneous generation of life from inorganic chemicals.

4. So-called vestigial remains, organs supposedly left over from a previous stage of evolutionary development (e.g., appendix or tonsils in man) often prove their usefulness and therefore are no firm evidence for macroevolution.

5. In regard to man, the evolutionary hypothesis fails to account satisfactorily for the origin of his spiritual nature (Gen. 2:7), and the argument of the survival of the fittest does not account for the artistic talents of man. Moreover, much of the anthropological evidence is very partial—partial skeletons and the discovery of skeletons without tools or primitive tools without skeletons. Skeletal reconstruction often is conjectural and sometimes open to considerable question.

Genesis and the Babylonian Creation Myth. Higher critics commonly have taught that the Genesis account of creation is a purified version of the Babylonian account, known as *Enuma Elish,* a cuneiform text of about one thousand lines on seven clay tablets. Although there are some similarities, the differences are vastly greater; the following should be especially noted.

1. *Enuma Elish* is not primarily a creation account. Its purpose is political: to advance the cause of Babylon in her bid for supremacy by portraying the preeminent place of her patron deity Marduk among the gods. It is essentially a hymn to Marduk.

2. *Enuma Elish* is grossly polytheistic; various gods share in the origin of things; Marduk himself is brought into existence by another god. Genesis posits an exalted monotheism with God as the creator of all things.

3. The gross mythology and inferior morals of *Enuma Elish* have no parallel in Genesis.

4. There is little parallel between the seven tablets and the seven creative days of Genesis. For instance, tablets 2 and 3 do not deal with any phase of creation.

5. In starting its account of creation with the existence of matter, *Enuma Elish* implies eternity of matter; Scripture teaches that God is a spirit who is the author of all matter-energy.

Anyone who makes even a cursory comparison of the two accounts will be tremendously impressed with the wide differences between them. It seems best to hold that any similarities arise from the fact that both accounts came from the same Semitic context and may be due to the fact that the human race once occupied a common home.[6]

NOTES

1. Edward J. Young, *Studies in Genesis* One (Philadelphia: Presbyterian & Reformed, 1964), p. 7, cf. pp. 1-14.
2. Harold J. Stigers, *A Commentary on Genesis* (Grand Rapids: Zondervan, 1976), p. 49.
3. Davis A. Young, *Creation and the Flood* (Grand Rapids: Baker, 1977), pp. 86-87.
4. Ibid., pp. 123-24.
5. Ibid., p. 128.
6. See Alexander Heidel, *The Babylonian Genesis*, 2d ed. (Chicago: U. of Chicago, 1951), pp. 130-40.

3

THE FALL OF MAN AND EXTENSION
OF CIVILIZATION

GENESIS 2:4–5:32

Even a quick and cursory survey of chapter 2 reveals its difference from chapter 1. Instead of terse, abrupt sentences, it has a more flowing style. Instead of God as the sovereign power of the universe (Elohim) it presents Him as the condescending, gracious God (Yahweh Elohim). Instead of a strictly chronological approach to creation, it concentrates on man as the crown of creation. Here, as subsequently in the book, there is movement from the general to the particular. This chapter is not to be construed as a product of a different author from chapter 1 and loosely joined to it, as critics commonly assert, but as a statement about creation with an entirely different purpose. Here the emphasis is on man, his mate, his environment and probation; all that is preparatory to a statement about his temptation and Fall.

Human Origin and Probation (2:4-25)

Early conditions (2:4-6). "These are the generations of" or "the beginnings of" introduces a new stage of the book. What follows concerns man in his relation to the newly-created "heavens and the earth." There is no question but that verses 5 and 6 picture the situation prior to man's creation and indicate the need for his creation in order that he might "till the ground." But there are two schools of thought as to how early in the creative process those verses fit. Some conclude that the process was essentially complete except for the appearance of man and some of the cultivated plants that appeared subsequently. Under that view the mist or subterranean streams rather than rain was the source of water supply for agriculture until the days of the Flood. Others believe that reference is to the condition of the earth after Genesis 1:2, before the creative process was very far advanced. Thus the atmosphere with its clouds and rainfall was not yet in existence; there was only a continual rise of mist over the watery waste. In any case, neither the wild grasses and weeds of the field nor cultivatable crops of the field had come into existence.

The creation of man (2:7). As a master craftsman God "formed" man, a fact that implies both skill and sovereignty. As the Creator He has the right to order the affairs of His creatures (cf. Isa. 29:16; Rom. 9:19-22). "From the dust of the ground" points to man's natural, chemical origin. The "breath of life," which God breathed into him to create a living being, involved more than animal life, because 1:27 made it clear that man was created in the image of God. Thus he was a moral, rational being capable of entering into fellowship with God. Both man's material and immaterial part came into being by direct divine initiative.

The provision of a habitat for man (2:8-17). Having created man, God prepared for him a beautiful place in which to live: a garden "in the east, in Eden," apparently related to the Sumerian *ēdin,* meaning *plain* or *steppe.* An effort is made to portray the garden as an actual, not a mythical, place. The garden is associated with four rivers, two of which are certainly known, the Euphrates and Hiddekel (Tigris), the great rivers of modern Iraq. Since the rivers apparently are named from east to west, the Pishon and Gihon must have flowed east of the Tigris. The Gihon is associated with the land of Cush, which therefore apparently should be located northeast of the head of the Persian Gulf, rather than in Ethiopia where the King James Version puts it. Havilah is linked with Cush in Genesis 10:7 and possibly was to the east of it. Presumably the garden was located somewhere in Mesopotamia. "Bdellium" (v. 12), a yellowish aromatic gum, may not be the correct intent of the Hebrew; onyx is also an uncertain translation; some suggest the stone may be lapis lazuli (a blue stone) instead. In that garden God provided ample nourishment, challenging occupation (vv. 15, 19), spiritual fellowship, and opportunity for cultural development (as the presence of gold and other resources implies).

God's planting of trees in the garden does not refer to original creation but to the furbishing of the garden. In addition He planted two special trees: the tree of life and the tree of knowledge of good and evil. What those trees were no one really knows. Evidently they were not magical trees and probably not poisonous either. It may well be, as many commentators suggest, that they were no different from other trees in the garden. But God set them up as a test of man's obedience to Him. He did not give any reason for the prohibition but simply enunciated it. Man was put on probation; the penalty for disobedience would be death, first moral and spiritual and later physical. The environment of man during his probation was magnificent indeed, hardly a setting contributing to his Fall. That fact argues cogently for the view that improving man's moral and social environment today would not necessarily make him a good person.

Creation of woman (2:18-25). The event about to be described actually took place on the sixth day of creation, as Genesis 1:27 makes clear. Likewise, the animals mentioned in verse 19 had been created earlier. The coming of animals and birds to Adam for naming demonstrates his dominion over creation, his knowledge, his power of speech, and the inadequacy of any of the lower forms of creation to serve as his proper companion. After it had been graphically demonstrated that there was no adequate complementary companion for Adam ("no helper fit for him"), God determined to provide one. God put Adam to sleep and took "one [or a piece] from his side," usually rendered "rib," and fashioned a woman from it. It may be instructive to note that God took something from the side of Adam, not from his head or his feet; for the woman was not to lord it over him nor to grovel at his feet but to walk by his side as his complementary partner. That complementary relationship is evident in the *Revised Standard Version's* rendering of verse 23: "This is at last bone of my bone"; the Hebrew for "bone" signifies not only body but "essence" or "self." After all the search throughout creation, at last one was found like Adam, "a fit helper"; and he gave her a name too: *woman.*

It is clear from Matthew 19:4-5 that the pronouncement of verse 24 was God's, not Adam's. He would not have been capable of such an observation at the time. The statement introduces important elements for a successful marriage: (1) a necessary degree of severance from parents so the couple can work out their own problems without interference; (2) a whole-hearted and permanent attachment to each other ("cleave"); and (3) a God-sealed bond and a sexual union ("one flesh"). Polygamy and adultery are ruled out.

26

GENESIS

The Fall of Man (3:1-24)

Temptation and disobedience (3:1-7). This passage provides the answer to another of the big questions of life: How do we account for the origin of sin and evil in the world? The Genesis record makes it clear that sin was not a part of God's original creation. Rather, it came as the result of the temptation of the first human pair, whom God had created with the power of choice. Man freely chose to rebel against God at the suggestion of an alien evil spirit. That spirit is not merely some impersonal force, but a powerful supernatural personality in conflict with God. His power is so tremendous that even the archangel Michael did not dare bring a judgment against him (Jude 9). Presumably Satan's own rebellion against God had occurred before the creation of the earth or at least before the creation of man.

Satan used as his instrument in the temptation the serpent apparently a very wonderful creature in its uncursed state. His approach was first to question whether God had not permitted Eve to eat of every tree of the garden. Perhaps he came to Eve with that doubt because she had gotten the prohibition secondhand. Adam heard the command directly from God and knew certainly the details of it. Eve had got the word from Adam and might have been made to question whether she had heard right. At any rate, Satan was able to concentrate on the prohibition and make her forget all the privileges she enjoyed in the garden. At least that was the implication of her reply; note that she omitted "all" or "every" in 3:2 and added "neither shall he touch it" in 3:3. In the latter case she seemed to be saying, "Not only can't we eat fruit of the tree of good and evil, we can't even touch it." Satan next moved on to declare categorically that God was wrong, that she would not die if she ate. And finally, he asserted that if she ate, she would become as God.

1) Eve's first major mistake was giving audience to Satan. Her 2) second error was consenting to linger and look on that which was forbidden. And she "saw that the tree was good for food," or appealed to the appetite (lust of the flesh, 1 John 2:16); "and that it was pleasant to the eyes" (lust of the eyes, 1 John 2:16); "and a tree to be desired to make one wise" (the pride or vainglory of life, 1 John 2:16). So her temptation was on the same pattern as

that with which Satan confronts human beings today and with which he confronted Christ in the wilderness (Matt. 4:1-11). Eve and Adam both ate of the fruit of the tree, and their eyes were opened—but only to see their shame and guilt. Eve was deceived, but Adam sinned knowingly (1 Tim. 2:14); why he did so, we can only speculate. Some suggest that he chose to stand by his wife; he preferred the woman to God. Adam knew what God had said, but he deliberately ate of the fruit because Eve asked him to do so. Therefore Adam's sin was greater than that of Eve, and the human race is said to have fallen in Adam and to have incurred death in him rather than in Eve (Rom. 5:12; 1 Cor. 15:22).

Sometimes questions are raised concerning why the Fall of man should hang on such an insignificant issue as eating a little fruit. Actually the sin was not in the eating but in the disobeying and rebelling prior to that act. The first pair chose to believe the word of Satan rather than the word of God and sought to elevate the will of man above the will of God. They wished to break the bounds of limitation imposed upon them and to become like God.

The eyes of Adam and Eve were opened, as Satan said they would be, but not in the way they had anticipated. The world at which they looked was spoiled as they projected evil onto innocence (Tit. 1:15). Once comfortable with each other, Adam and Eve were now ill at ease; their experience was something of a foregleam of fallen human relations in general. "They knew they were naked" and wove or plaited loincloths made from leaves to hide their shame. They now knew evil experientially with all of its attendant guilt, sorrow, shame, and misery. The age of innocence had ended.

Divine confrontation (3:8-13). Next God came in grace, seeking fallen man. Adam and Eve heard "the sound," not "the voice" of God. Taking on human characteristics, God seemed to push aside branches and undergrowth and to make the sound of footsteps as He came walking through the garden in the time of day when cool breezes of evening began to blow. Fellowship that previously had been a joy was broken, and the prospect of meeting God brought terror. Adam and Eve hid themselves. Yahweh Elohim, the covenant-redemptive God, sought them out. It is interesting that Satan and Eve had called Him only Elohim. Adam confessed his plight: "I was afraid . . . I was naked . . . I hid." Estranged from God, he sought to avoid contact with Him—a natural result of spiritual death. Through a process of questioning, God tried to lead Adam to make a full confession of guilt. But he did that only partially; Adam quickly utilized a trick of fallen human nature: "passing the buck." Not only did Adam try to weasel out of a bad situation by blaming Eve, but he also tried to blame God Himself for his predicament: "the woman whom You gave me." Apparently without any response to Adam's comments, God turned to Eve to elicit a confession from her. She learned quickly; following the lead of Adam, she put the whole blame on the serpent.

Divine judgment (3:14-19). Next God turned to Satan. This time there were no rhetorical questions. The one ultimately responsible must pay the ultimate penalty. Satan's agent of the temptation was cursed. From a beautiful, upright, highly intelligent creature, the serpent was degraded into a loathsome reptile that would "bite the dust" forever. Then to Satan himself He delivered what often is called the *protevangelium* or "first gospel" (v. 15). The enmity between Satan and the woman showed that he was not the friend he had pretended to be at the time of the temptation; Satan was really the enemy of mankind. "The seed of the woman" in a general way comprehends the children of God, whereas "seed of the serpent" denotes the unregenerate part of mankind that will be in conflict with the seed of the woman down through the millennia. But more specifically, the seed of the woman is masculine singular in the original: "*he* shall crush your head"; "you will bruise his heel." The seed of the woman especially points to Christ and His coming to earth (Gal. 4:4). Satan would bruise His heel, achieve His crucifixion. But in that crucifixion He (Christ) would judge Satan (Col. 2:14-15) and rise again, making it possible for believers to triumph over evil forces (Rom. 16:20) and laying the basis on which Christ ultimately will defeat Satan according to the book of Revelation. On the cross Jesus Christ would pay the price of man's sin and make redemption available for the entire race.

In addition to the general judgment on humanity involving spiritual and physical death for disobedience to God, there were specific curses. Motherhood would be accompanied by great suffering and personal danger. And because the woman had persuaded the man to do what she wanted and he had eaten forbid-

den fruit with her in the Fall, often she would find herself in difficult situations in interpersonal relations with him. She might find
herself in a servile yearning for him that Stigers interprets as
occasionally amounting to nymphomania.[1] And man's lordship
over woman might be exploitive to the point of physical degrada-
tion and slavery.

Man would have his set of trials, too. He was condemned to
exhausting labor to make a living; that toil was made more difficult by a curse on nature that will continue until the end times
(Rom. 8:20-23). The need to work often is looked on as a result
of the Fall, but such is not the case. Adam was very busy before
the Fall, fulfilling the responsibility to "till" and "care for" (NEB)*
the garden. The Fall brought on a new kind of labor with its
many agonies. No doubt plant diseases, drought, floods, hurri-
canes, and other disasters leading to shortages and even starvation were in view. Exhausting toil with its many unpleasantries
was to continue throughout life. And ultimately man would die,
as God had warned would be the case. Postponement of death
did not eliminate its inevitability.

Divine provision and expulsion (3:20-24). Adam called his
wife's name "Eve," meaning "life" or "life source," because he
recognized her as the mother of all living. In its simplest significance, that observation could merely indicate that Adam recognized his wife would be the mother of all human descendants to
follow. But coming after the severe curses and the pronouncement
of death in previous verses, it sounds more like some sort of statement of faith or hope. And thus it may indicate that Adam looked
forward to the coming of that seed of woman who would undo
the fiasco he had brought on humanity. If so, his statement reflects
a certain awareness of divine provision.

Another evidence of divine provision involved the killing of animals to make more permanent clothing for mankind. That not
only met a human need but it also put a divine stamp on the wear-
ing of clothing. And possibly it inaugurated the inclusion of meat
in human diet. To foresee the atonement here may involve too
much of an assumption. There is no reference to the erection of
an altar and the offering of sacrifices.

The curse on man was finalized with the expulsion from the

New English Bible.

Garden of Eden. Once man was driven from the garden, cheru-
bim, angelic beings especially designated to protect the holiness
of God, were stationed at the gate to prevent reentry (cf. Ezek.
1:4-16; 10:5). The reason given for expulsion was to prevent man
from eating of the tree of life. Commentators generally observe
that the tree could not possibly bear fruit capable of reversing
the effects of Adam's sin. What was it then? Wood argues that
it had symbolic value, symbolizing life that would have been man's
if he had been obedient. Preventing him from eating would symbolize the death he had incurred because of disobedience and
the impossibility of regaining paradise.[2] Moreover, in eating of
the tree man might have developed the false notion that by that
means he was capable of perpetuating physical life or of contributing something to his spiritual redemption. To prevent the rise
of such false views God had to expel man from the garden.

Effects of the Fall and Extension of Civilization (4:1-24)

Cain and Abel (4:1-15). Speculations about whether children
were born in the Garden of Eden before the expulsion, or about
the length of the period of probation, or whether Cain was the
firstborn, are fruitless. Scripture implies that Cain was the firstborn. If he was not, Eve seems to have centered some special
hope in him: "I have gotten a man with [the help of] God." She
had a sense of working with God in bringing about that birth, and
viewed Cain as a special gift from God. Perhaps he would somehow contribute to the realization of the hope of Genesis 3:15.
Later Eve had another son, Abel. While they were growing up,
and perhaps even between them, other sons and daughters must
have been born. God had told Eve that He would greatly multiply
her conception (Gen. 3:16). Probably for a long time children
were born every year or two. The degenerative effects of sin on
the human body had not yet become evident. Thus the ability of
women to have large families and the danger of men marrying
their sisters (as in the case of Cain and Abel and others) were
not then issues.

Farming and sheep herding appear as the earliest means of
human livelihood. It seems unwise to read into the account a
rivalry between the two ways of life. "In the process of time" may
be viewed as an indefinite time reference, but here seems to indi-

cate some sacred anniversary when Adam and all his posterity
gathered at the primitive sanctuary for worship. Attention centers
on Cain and Abel. Each brought a *minḥâ*, an offering or gift of
homage or allegiance, that was natural for him. Cain brought
agricultural produce and Abel the "best of the firstlings of his
flock." God accepted Abel's offering but rejected Cain's. Why is
a debated question. In the passage itself the intimation is that
Abel brought his best whereas Cain may have been somewhat in-
different or careless. The New Testament indicates further that
Cain's life was characterized by evil and Abel's by righteousness.
In other words, Cain's offering did not proceed from a heart right
toward God (1 John 3:12; cf. Matt. 23:35; Heb. 11:4; 12:24; Jude
11). Proverbs 21:27 is instructive at this point: "The sacrifice of
the wicked is an abomination." It is additionally possible that
Cain was scored for not offering a blood sacrifice, as commentators
often claim; but Scripture does not say that, and by no means did
all the sacrifices even in the Mosaic system require the shedding
of blood.

How God's pleasure or displeasure was demonstrated is not
clear, but apparently it was public; and all knew the verdict. The
public affront wounded Cain's pride and made him angry. Stigers
translates the end of verse 5, "angry because of chagrin."[3] Then
God began to remonstrate with or reason with Cain. He said in
effect that if Cain did well or right, if his heart was right before
God, and if he offered the right offering, he too would be accepted.
If he refused to bow before God in true contrition, then sin like a
besieger would be at the door; it would be "eager to be at you"
(Moffatt), to overpower you, "but you must master it" (RSV).
If he allowed himself to continue to be consumed emotionally by
his anger and feeling of rejection, he was on a dangerous course
indeed. How dangerous becomes immediately apparent. Cain
evidently paid no attention to God.

The division of the text is abrupt. A common way of dealing
with verse 8 is the approach of the RSV: "Cain said to Abel his
brother, 'Let us go out to the field.'" The conclusion of the RSV
translators and other Old Testament scholars is that a phrase has
dropped out of the Hebrew text: "Let us go out to the field." That
is supplied from the Samaritan Pentateuch, the Septuagint (Greek
translation of the Old Testament), the Syriac, and Latin Vulgate.

Thus Cain became guilty of premeditated murder. When Cain got Abel out in the field he killed him, probably from jealousy and hurt pride, and no doubt buried him.

Probably on the way back home God accosted Cain. In response to the question of where Abel was, Cain responded with a barefaced lie, "I don't know." With his lie he coupled a defiant attitude and a callous selfishness that reflected a sin-seared conscience (1 Tim. 4:2): "Am I my brother's keeper?" Of course God did not need a confession from the criminal to discover the details of the crime. God said in effect, "Each drop of your brother's blood screams out the testimony of your guilt and cries to me for vindication." God's judgment was swift: any land Cain tried to till would not yield an increase to him, and he would be a fugitive and wanderer.

Overwhelmed with the magnitude of the judgment, Cain said, "My punishment is greater than I can bear" (v. 13). Although this passage is capable of other renderings, in this case the King James and RSV translations are to be preferred because he was overcome with the severity of the sentence more than a sense of his guilt. Then Cain proceeded to itemize the elements in the judgment as he now felt it: driven away from his home, cut off from the grace of God, banished as a wanderer, and the object of vengeance killing. In grace God responded with care even for the sinner. He put a mark upon him to provide something of a safe conduct. What the mark was no one knows, and it did not protect against attack or even death by assault but involved a deterrent in the warning that anyone killing Cain would suffer a worse death.

Extension of Cainite Civilization (4:16-24). With no word of repentance, Cain went out from the presence of God to dwell in the land of Nod ("wandering"), east of Edom. The place is not known, and it may not have been a definite locality at all. The following verses describe the development of civilization among the descendants of Cain, presumably to mitigate the effects of the curse. The building of a city, evidently an organized village (v. 17), would help to solve the problem of wandering. Jubal's developments in music (v. 21) would help to bring some sort of enjoyment to unhappy people, and Tubal-cain's contributions in metallurgy (v. 22) would alleviate to a degree the drudgery of

labor. The metal working of that early period dated long before the historical bronze and iron ages. Probably that prediluvian
culture was wiped out by the Flood and metallurgical techniques
had to be discovered or learned all over again in the later period.
The materialistic success of Cainite civilization did not fill the
spiritual void or meet the real needs of society.

Evidently violence too was characteristic of that branch of
Adam's descendants. In verse 23 Lamech, the first polygamist,
calls his wives to obtain their approval of his killing in self-defense
of a lad who had wounded him. Here a distinction is made between premeditated murder (Abel's) and unpremeditated killing
in self-defense (the lad's). And Lamech observed that if one taking vengeance on Cain was to suffer sevenfold punishment, then
one taking vengeance on him should suffer seventy-sevenfold
(seventy times seven, Matt. 18:21-22, meaning *to the fullest*), perhaps capital punishment.

The Godly Line of Seth (4:25—5:32)

Probably soon after Abel's murder and Cain's banishment, Eve
gave birth to another son, whom she named *Seth* ("appointed").
In so naming him, Eve acted in faith, for she believed God had
given her a replacement for Abel: that He had "appointed me
another seed instead of Abel." Then God blessed and comforted
the parents who had lost two children, the one by violent death
and the other by banishment. The mention of "another seed" seems
to refer again to the promise and hope of Genesis 3:15. The observation that Seth was born when Adam was 130 (5:3) shows how
truncated the narrative really is. The human family must have
been very numerous indeed by that time. But the descendants of
Cain had no interest in God whatever, and apparently the rest of
Adam's progeny were not much better. God started over again
with the godly line of Seth.

During the days of Seth's son Enos, "Men began to call on the
name of Yahweh" (deity as a covenant-keeping and redemptive
God). This must refer to some sort of spiritual quickening and
may indicate the first revival. Perhaps some Cainites as well as
Sethites were involved.

Though 5:1 purports to give the genealogy of Adam, actually
Seth's line is highlighted as the true line of descent from Adam.

Several general observations need to be made about this chapter. (1) Human history is traced down to Noah the deliverer. (2) The disastrous effects of the Fall are underscored with the repetition of "and he died." But one was missing from the morgue: Enoch, who walked wih God. (3) Efforts to explain the extended lengths of life in some way other than the literal sense have proved completely unsatisfactory, and those figures evidently must be taken in the literal sense. A tradition of human longevity before the Flood does exist in Mesopotamian literature. (4) On the basis of both historical investigation and internal evidence from Scripture itself, the general conclusion today is that biblical genealogies are not designed to be complete but include only representative names in the line of the Redeemer. The line of the Redeemer is carefully highlighted here, for even though each descendant of Seth evidently had several sons, only the one in the Messianic line is named.

Archaeological and historical studies keep pushing back the date of the origin of man and the beginnings of culture beyond any computed according to the view that there are no gaps in the biblical genealogies. And studies of the genealogies themselves show they are not complete. For example, the genealogy of Christ in Matthew 1 is put together in a symmetrical fashion: fourteen generations from Abraham to David (about 1000 years), fourteen generations from David to the Captivity (about 400 years), and fourteen generations from the Captivity to Christ (600 years). In Matthew 1:8 Joram is said to have begotten Uzziah (Ozias) when actually three kings were omitted between the two. "Beget" and "son of" were used in a much different way in Semitic circles from what they are today. One might "beget" a grandson or descendant, and a "son of" might be merely a descendant of.[4] But even if one holds to the view that there are no gaps in the biblical genealogies, one cannot be dogmatic about a date of origins because chronological systems based on that view hold dates for the creation of Adam diverging by several thousand years.

Chapter 5 begins with a reminder that Elohim (reversion now to God as sovereign and omnipotent) had created man in His own likeness. He created them male and female and called them *Adam,* a generic term equivalent to the English "person." In time Adam came to be used as the personal name of the first man.

Adam's creation in the likeness or image of God was a perfect creation. Seth's birth in the likeness of Adam involved not only fully human characteristics but also the inheritance of Adam's corrupt sin nature. That fallen nature was doomed to death, despite Satan's assertion, "You shall not surely die" (Gen. 3:4). Chapter 5 abundantly demonstrates that fact with its recurring refrain, "and he died."

But Enoch never went through death. A particularly devout man who walked with God, "he was not; for God took him." Though some have sought to water down that statement and make it refer to something less than being caught away into heaven alive, Hebrews 11:5 is very specific: "Enoch was translated that he should not see death." The New Testament also fills in another aspect of Enoch's life. He functioned as a prophet, condemning the ungodliness of his society and predicting that ultimately the Lord would return in judgment on the ungodly and their evil deeds (Jude 14-15).

Another outstanding person in the genealogy was Lamech, who had a son whom he called Noah (meaning rest), because by faith he envisioned him as giving "comfort . . . concerning our work." Lamech's reference to Genesis 3:17 seems to put "comfort" on a purely physical level, but any person viewed as giving relief from the curse on nature ought to be thought of as fulfilling in some way the hope of Genesis 3:15. The hope of spiritually-minded Lamech was destined to be fulfilled in a way he would never have dreamed, however. Noah would indeed bring rest and comfort to the righteous who had suffered at the hands of their corrupt society. Through him that society would be wiped out.

NOTES

1. Harold G. Stigers, A Commentary on Genesis (Grand Rapids: Zondervan, 1976), p. 80.
2. Leon J. Wood, Genesis (Grand Rapids: Zondervan, 1975), p. 37.
3. Stigers, p. 86.
4. For a discussion of the question of gaps in the biblical chronology, see Oswald T. Allis, The Five Books of Moses (Philadelphia: Presbyterian & Reformed, 1943), pp. 261-64; Gleason Archer, Survey of Old Testament Introduction, 2d rev. ed. (Chicago: Moody, 1973), pp. 185-89; Merrill F. Unger, Introductory Guide to the Old Testament (Grand Rapids: Zondervan, 1951), pp. 192-94; and B. B. Warfield, Studies in Theology (New York: Oxford, 1932), pp. 235-58.

4

THE FLOOD

GENESIS 6:1—9:29

As the waters surged around Noah's ark, so debate surges around almost every aspect of the Flood account. Even the most reverent Bible student who accepts the Genesis account as historical is left with numerous unanswered questions. All the efforts of modern scholarship have settled little. We still do not know exactly why the Flood came, the nature of the ark, the size of the ark, the physical causes of the Flood, the extent of the Flood, or even where the ark landed. But lack of certainty does not eliminate the necessity of looking at the problems.

Why the Flood Came (6:1-7)

On the face of it, this passage teaches that God brought on the judgment of the Flood because of extreme wickedness; but there the agreement stops. In the midst of rapid population growth, the "sons of God" took wives from among the "daughters of men." One school of interpretation holds that the former must be angels and the latter human beings. A second teaches that the former were Sethites and the latter Cainites. Other views have inconsequential followings and need not be commented on here.

In favor of the view that the "sons of God" were angels is the argument that in the Old Testament "sons of God" refers exclusively to angels (e.g., Job 1:6; 2:1; 38:7). Moreover, two New Testament passages seem to support the idea. In 2 Peter 2:4-6 the sin of angels is mentioned just before judgment on the world by a flood. And Jude 5-7 does appear to condemn angels for leaving their normal limitations and getting involved in the sexual sins of Sodom and Gomorrah. But by way of answer, Christ specifically declared that angels cannot marry (Matt. 22:30; Mark 12:25). Moreover, angels do not appear in the first five chapters of the book, nor do they appear clearly in this context. And it is strange that judgment would fall on man alone for the sin committed when angels presumably bore the primary guilt.

In favor of the view that the "sons of God" were from the godly line of Seth is the fact that a godly line has been described in chapter 4; the idea that believers are sons of God is common in the Old Testament (usually Israel is said to be "the sons of God"); and warnings against marriage between believers and unbelievers are also common in the Old Testament. But that interpretation does not deal adequately with the fact that "sons of God" commonly refers to angels in the Old Testament and that the term "daughters of men" has no specific or technical connotation.

Many interpreters come out dogmatically in favor of one of the above views, but in light of all the evidence it seems impossible to do so. Furthermore, it is not even possible to discover the specific sin referred to in verse 2. It may be that angels overstepped their bounds, or that men used no spiritual discrimination in choosing mates, or that polygamy was involved. Nor is it clear whether the giants of verse 4a are to be regarded as offspring of the marriages referred to or whether they were present before the marriages took place; commentators again divide on the issue. The offspring of unions mentioned in 4b were "mighty men," strong in battle, and "men of renown," known for their various talents. Coming in this context, reference must be to abilities that were misapplied for the corruption of society.

In contrast to the creation narrative when God saw that all was "good," God now saw the great wickedness in the earth, so great that every "purpose" or "impulse" of man was evil "continually" (Rom. 7:18). Describing His reaction in human terms, God "regretted" that He had created man and determined to wipe out the fauna and human life of the earth. But God established a grace period of 120 years (v. 3), during which time Noah as a "preacher of righteousness" (2 Pet. 2:5) built an ark (1 Pet. 3:20).

God's Gracious Provision (6:8-22)

Noah found favor with God. "Righteous," right with God, and "perfect," of unimpeachable character, he "walked with God" as Enoch had. In that close walk with God he enjoyed God's friendship and came to know "what his lord does" (John 15:15). As with Abraham, friendship with God let him in on a secret of de-

struction. Whereas Abraham learned of the destruction of Sodom
and the other cities of the plain (Gen. 18:17-32), Noah found out
about the destruction of the world.

Earlier the source of evil in the earth had been noted (intermarriage, however interpreted); now the universality of corruption is underscored. Corruption, violence, and anarchy were rife,
and humanity was responsible for corrupting its own way (v. 12).
Moreover, the report of how bad things were did not arise from
hearsay; God in His omniscience scanned the earth (v. 12) and
knew fully the depths of corruption into which men had sunk.

In grace God now moved to rescue Noah and his family from
the judgment that was to fall on the earth. He instructed Noah to
build an ark of gopher wood (possibly cypress, cedar, or oak,
presently unidentified) that should be adequately caulked with
bitumen. It was to measure 300 cubits long by 50 cubits broad
and 30 cubits high. The length of that cubit is not certainly known;
but taking the smallest likely measurement, about eighteen inches,
the ark would have been about 450 feet by 75 feet by 45 feet,
with a displacement of about 15,000 tons. The vessel was to have
three decks, a door in the side, and a window, which is commonly
interpreted as an opening a cubit high under the eave and running
around the entire structure. In response to those who doubt that
Noah could have had the expertise to build such a great ocean-
going vessel, it needs only to be observed that the ark was much
more like a great barge than a modern ocean liner.

Because God planned to bring a flood on the earth that would
destroy all terrestrial life, Noah was to take aboard his wife, his
three sons and their wives, a pair each of all birds and animals
(later expanded, 7:2), and food for the livestock and people.
"Shall come to you" (v. 20) indicates that God would impel the
fauna to come to Noah at the right time. He would not have to
move about the earth trying to catch them. How many individual fauna may have been involved is not known because there is
no way of determining whether parent types (dog, cat, cow) or
more numerous representations were intended. Some 4,100 species
of mammals and some 8,600 species of birds exist on earth today.

The first mention of covenant in the Bible appears in verse 18
and is elaborated in chapter 9. The covenant was made with
righteous Noah and through him would extend to his family and

beyond. To be sure, the covenant would guarantee his physical preservation but would lead on to the beginning of a new age.

Again it is clear how very abbreviated the biblical narrative really is. Noah was 500 when he "began to beget" Shem, Ham, and Japheth (5:32); he was 600 when the Flood began (7:6). It seems rather unlikely that no other children were born to Noah before the age of 500, or that none were born to any of his sons before the age of 100. Did Noah and his sons have other children who refused to follow in the steps of their parents and were swept away by prevailing evil? Possibly they did, but the text does not tell us. Nor does it say whether Noah's sons helped their father during most of the construction process.

Boarding the Ark (7:1-9, 13-16)

The ark was completed. Cages for birds and animals were in place. Food supplies had been laid in. God issued the gracious instruction to board. Basically all was made possible because of the faith of righteous Noah (7:1); "righteousness delivers from death" (Prov. 10:2; 11:6). Noah was one of God's great heroes of faith (Heb. 11:7). He stood alone against the whole condemned world and took its ridicule for 120 years while he built the ark. No doubt his building activity itself was to be viewed as the primary element in his preaching of righteousness (2 Pet. 2:5). With every day of construction he proclaimed the judgment of God against sin and the grace of God in offering deliverance.

Instructions for saving creatures (6:19-20) were amplified (7:2-3), and details would be repeated on fulfillment (7:8-9). God's careful provision and sovereign control of the operation are evident in those statements. Moreover, the matter-of fact specifications about preservation of life and the careful notations of time throughout the Flood account help to establish its factual, historical character. Poetic, symbolic, and mythical elements are missing.

Throughout this passage the faith and obedience of Noah are striking: "Noah did according to all that God commanded him" (6:22; 7:5); "Noah went in" (7:7). But so are the sovereign initiatives of God ("God commanded," 7:5, 9, 16; "God said," 7:1) and the submissive response of nature ("there went in unto Noah," 7:9, 15-16).

It seems that pairs of all animals were to be saved (6:19-20).

Seven pairs of clean animals or animals designated for food were to be taken on board the ark (7:2). (Some translate "seven of every kind" [e.g., NIV*], with the seventh one being part of the sacrifice after the Flood.) Naturally larger numbers of such animals would be needed. No doubt unclean animals were preserved to maintain balance in the ecostructure. Evidently differences between clean and unclean animals were recognized early in human history, but restrictive religious control on eating unclean animals and birds was not spelled out until Moses' day. Studies utilizing a variety of estimates of the size of the ark and the number of animals to be housed on it demonstrate that it was indeed large enough for the animals and their provisions. If some of the larger ones went into hibernation, they would have required less space to move around.

After God's invitation to Noah and his family to enter the ark, He predicted the beginning of the Flood seven days hence. Thus all deliberate speed, but no panic effort, was to be exercised to get the animals on board. When at the end of seven days all were on board, everything was in readiness for judgment to fall. God, who Himself had been in charge of the whole operation, shut them in, and the rains began.

Flood on the Earth (7:10-12, 17—8:14)

Physical cause of the Flood. Clearly the Flood came because of heavy rains. A literal translation of the Hebrew is graphic: "the sluice gates of heaven were opened" (7:11). It rained so hard that it was as if someone had opened the sluice gates in the dam of heaven and allowed all the waters held in reserve to gush forth on the earth. Additionally, "the springs of the great deep were cleft asunder" (7:11). Exactly what that means is not clear. Often it is interpreted to say that some convulsion of the earth's crust released stores of subterranean waters. But to date geologists have been unable to find evidence of such subterranean reserves or of any general and cataclysmic alteration of the earth's crust that may have eliminated such reservoirs by the collapse of geological structures above them.

Extent of the Flood. As one reads the Flood narrative in English, the Flood appears to have been universal. For example, "all

New International Version.

flesh died" (7:21), and the mountains were covered with water to a depth of fifteen cubits (at least 21 feet, 7:20). Belief in a universal flood is the traditional view, but numerous arguments for a local flood have been raised. (1) The Hebrew word translated "land" or "earth" could have a purely local reference (e.g., 7:10, 17-19). (2) If the waters were to cover all the highest mountains in the world, even if they were not so high as they now stand, several times more water would be required than now exists on earth. (3) The problem is not solved by suggesting that the water evaporated into the atmosphere or returned to subterranean cavities, because neither or both could hold more than a small fraction of it. (4) Most plant life would have been destroyed by submersion under salt water for a year. (5) Presumably most of the marine life would have been killed off by the Flood, as a result of dilution of salt waters of the oceans or starved by the disturbance or loss of normal feeding grounds. Some have sought to solve that problem by observing that today there is a certain layering in the oceans; the percentage of salts in solution and other conditions are not the same at all levels.

But weight of evidence is not all one-sided. Numerous arguments also have been advanced in favor of a universal flood. (1) The phrase "under the whole heaven" (7:19) presumably cannot be reduced to apply to a local condition. (2) A local flood would not have fulfilled the purpose of judging the sinfulness of the entire antediluvian population, unless, of course, all human beings were then living in a limited locale. (3) An ark would have been unnecessary because both animals and human beings could have fled the Mesopotamian valley and returned when the Flood was over. (4) The promise never again to destroy all flesh (terrestrial) with a flood (9:11) has universal implications. (5) A flood that would cover the Ararat Mountains (17,000 feet) could not be a local flood. Water seeks its own level, and would flow over the entire earth to a depth of three miles. (6) Universality of flood legends among the people of the world seems to require a universal flood.

If one is to take seriously or literally the various features of the Flood narrative (e.g., size of ark, depth of floodwaters, purpose of bringing judgment on all mankind), one will find it hard to accept a purely local flood. But as a matter of fact there are problems with either view.

Duration of the Flood. The average person thinks of the Flood as having lasted forty days because that is the length of time it rained hard. But Noah and his family and the animals were actually shut up in the ark for a total of 371 days; they entered on the seventeenth day of the second month of Noah's six hundredth year (7:11) and disembarked on the twenty-seventh day of the second month of Noah's six hundred first year (8:13-14). The chronology of the year in the ark is as follows. Immediately after God shut the door of the ark, rain cascaded onto the earth for forty days and nights, and water rapidly covered the earth. Then it continued to rain lightly for another 110 days. This conclusion is reached from Genesis 8:4 and 8:2, where it stated that God stopped the rain 150 days after it began on the seventeenth day of the seventh month (five 30-day months after it began, 7:11); thus the 150 days of 7:24 must be viewed as including two periods of forty and one hundred ten days.

For the next seventy-four days the waters abated until the tops of the mountains could be seen (from the seventeenth day of the seventh month until the first day of the tenth month = 13 + 30 + 30 + 1, Gen. 8:5). Forty days later Noah released a raven (8:6-7), which did not return because it was able to scavenge for its food. Seven days later (determined from the "other seven days" of v. 10 and the total of v. 14), Noah sent out a dove, which found no resting place and returned (v. 9). Seven days later yet he sent out a dove that returned with an olive leaf (v. 11). After another seven days Noah sent out a dove the third time, and it did not return (v. 12). After an additional twenty-nine-day lapse Noah removed the covering of the ark (v. 14). After yet another fifty-seven days God commanded Noah to evacuate the ark (vv. 14-17). All those figures together (150 + 74 + 40 + 7 + 7 + 7 + 29 + 57) total 371.

Disembarkation from the Ark (8:15-22)

"And Noah went forth." Noah and his family would never forget the moment they pushed open the door of the ark and walked out. A spine-tingling moment it was! There was no sign of human and animal life anywhere on the horizon. They emerged into an empty world, stripped bare by the hand of God that had gestured in judgment. After a year of walking the bare planks of the decks of the ark, soft grass underfoot was such a delight. And what wonderful air to breathe, thoroughly washed by the scouring hand of God and now completely unpolluted! It would never be so pure again. The bright sunlight was blinding to eyes accustomed to the dimly-lit rooms of the ark.

But Noah was not merely carried away with the exhilaration of the moment. Immediately he remembered the goodness of God in preserving him and his family through catastrophic judgment and in singling out them alone to assume the responsibility of repeopling the earth. In gratitude Noah built an altar and sacrificed on it one each of every clean animal and bird. God accepted the offering and promised never again to blot out all living things "as I have done," in the manner He had just done, that is, by flood. The seasons that had been obliterated for a year were now promised in regularity until the end of time.

Verse 21 creates a problem as translated in most versions. It seems to say that God would not curse the ground because man was evil—rewarding good for evil. The idea presented in the Hebrew original is rather that God would not levy such a devastating curse again "though" man is evil. The New English Bible properly conveys the meaning: "Never again will I curse the ground because of man, however evil his inclinations may be."

"The Lord smelled the pleasing odor." Of course God's righteous demands were not met merely by the offering of animal sacrifice. The heart of the offender must be right if God is to accept the sacrifice. That is clear from numerous passages in the Old Testament, but none puts the truth more forcefully than Isaiah 1: "I delight not in the blood of bullocks, or of lambs, or of he goats" (v. 11); "Bring no more vain oblations" (v. 13); "Wash you, make you clean; put away the evil of your doings" (v. 16). Moreover, blood sacrifices would be only a temporary expedient, an anticipatory expedient, to be done away when the once-for-all sacrifice of Christ should satisfy the just demands of God (Heb. 9:16-28).

The Genesis and Babylonian Flood Accounts. As with the Creation account, higher critics of the Old Testament have tended to treat the Flood as a Hebrew myth, perhaps borrowed from Babylonian sources and purified of some of its crassest elements. The

story appeared on the eleventh tablet of a twelve-tablet account,
the *Gilgamesh Epic*, which tells of Gilgamesh's search for immortality. In the narrative Gilgamesh (king of Uruk, biblical Erech)
interviewed Utnapishtim, the "Babylonian Noah," and learned
from him the story of the Flood and his securing of immortality.

The differences between the two accounts are far greater than
the similarities. (1) The Babylonian story is grossly polytheistic,
whereas the Genesis narrative is monotheistic. (2) The Mesopotamian deluge came because man was so noisy that the god Enlil
could not sleep; so he decided to destroy man. The Genesis account gives the sin of man as the cause of the Flood. (3) In the
Gilgamesh Epic an effort is made to hide from man the coming of
the Flood, whereas the biblical account gives abundant opportunity to repent. (4) Utnapishtim's ship was cubical, had seven
stories, and was much larger than Noah's. (5) The duration of the
Babylonian flood was different; Utnapishtim endured a rain lasting
only seven days and nights. (6) Utnapishtim was granted immortality whereas Noah was not. There are also numerous minor
differences.

Scholars increasingly find the view that the Hebrews borrowed
from the Babylonian account unacceptable because it fails to
account for the differences between the two. More appealing is
the position that both descended from a common original. After
all, Mesopotamia was the original home of the Hebrews, and the
place where civilization made a fresh start after the Flood. What
would be more likely than that many accounts of an early tragedy
of such magnitude would be preserved by peoples who lived in
Mesopotamia or had migrated from there? A high view of inspiration does not rule out the use of source materials; it only guarantees accuracy of the finished product.

Noah's Life after the Flood (9:1-29)

God's commandments to Noah and his sons (9:1-7). God's commandments to Noah are reminiscent of those He gave to Adam.
But the tone and atmosphere are different. The heavy pall of sin
now hangs over all relationships. Strife and murder are to be expected in the natural order. With the earth depopulated, a new
progeny was essential (cf. v. 7); so God commanded Noah and his
sons, "Be fruitful, multiply, and fill the earth." Though nothing is

said in this passage about procreation for the glory of God, that must be intended. Certainly God was not concerned merely with having people on the earth. He had just wiped out the masses because of their sin. In subsequent generations He would again and again score individuals and communities for their waywardness. Evidently as those new people were brought into the world they were to be taught the fear of God.

The dominion of man over all creation is reaffirmed in verse 2, but there are differences from God's original statement to Adam. Instead of the harmony of the original creation, the Creator now instills a "fear" and "dread" or "terror" in the fauna of earth to prevent them from destroying human beings. God's second command extends man's domain over creation to include meat in his diet. But there is a prohibition, that all blood be properly drained from animals slain for food. Probably that restriction is at least in part an anticipation of the later, more fully developed sacrificial system. Since life resides in the blood itself (Lev. 17:11), the use of blood was to be sacred in sacrifice and not be consumed by man (Lev. 7:27; 17:10). The pouring out of the blood of sacrificial animals temporarily covered the sins of humanity and looked forward to the time when Christ's shedding of His blood would forever remove the penalty of human sin.

A third command concerns the shedding of human blood. The sanctity of man's blood is stressed in verses 5 and 6, especially because he was created in the image of God. Though the moral image may have been flawed greatly in the Fall or even viewed as destroyed, the natural image remains. Therefore, a human being is to be especially respected, and the shedding of his blood is a crime against God Himself, against His majesty and government. God intrudes into the administration of justice: "For your lifeblood I will surely demand an accounting. I will demand an accounting from every animal. And from each man, too, I will demand an accounting . . ." (v. 5, NIV). God Himself might exact punishment, but normally He would do so through a constituted authority. In very simple phraseology He instituted capital punishment: "Whoever shed's a man's blood, by men shall his blood be shed." Of course a beast that kills a man is to be put to death (e.g., Exodus 21:28), but the focus of attention here is on human beings. God does not merely permit execution for taking a human life but commands it: "shall be shed" must be rendered in the imperative. "By men shall his blood be shed" is left unspecific at that point but must refer to judicial execution by constituted government when it would be set up at a later time. Elaboration of regulations connected with capital punishment appears in such passages as Exodus 21:12-29 and Numbers 35:10-34. Failure to administer capital punishment pollutes a land, according to Numbers 35:33-34; and the implication is that such continued pollution may bring on dire consequences.

God's covenant with Noah and his sons (9:8-17). God next made a covenant, a binding form of divine promise, with Noah and his sons to the effect that never again would He destroy all living creatures or ruin the earth with a flood. The covenant was unconditional and unmerited. In that brute beasts were also its beneficiaries, understanding of the covenant was not even necessary for it to have force. Moreover, no obligations were laid on the recipients to guarantee avoidance of universal catastrophe by water; and the covenant was to be everlasting. The sign of the covenant was to be the rainbow, which may or may not have come into existence at that time. Some argue that there is no reason why a rainbow could not have appeared earlier because even a mist can produce a rainbow (if one holds that there was no rain prior to the Flood). Others conclude that atmospheric conditions did indeed change after the Flood and that the rainbow would be a much more effective sign of God's grace and providence if it were a new phenomenon. In any case, all the text requires is that God was now setting or appointing the rainbow (whether or not pre-existent) as a sign of His everlasting covenant and that every time it appeared it would serve as a reminder to God of the covenant He had made and to man of the providence and power of God. The rainbow still served as a portrayal of the glory of God to Ezekiel about 600 B.C. (Ezek. 1:28) and to the apostle John about A.D. 100 (Rev. 4:3).

The future of the races foretold (9:18-27). The primary theme of this passage is the unity of mankind and the prophetic future of the races. Noah's drunkenness is only a secondary theme and somewhat incidental to the whole flow of events. The sons of Noah as progenitors of the three great divisions of the human race now are introduced. Wherever they are mentioned in Scripture, the order is Shem, Ham, and Japheth; and it may be assumed that they are listed in the order of their age, Shem being the oldest. Ham is identified as father of Canaan, in anticipation of events about to be related. Verse 19 is precise in indicating that those three sons of Noah were the ones from whom the earth was re-populated. During the 350 years that Noah lived after the Flood, he did not father additional sons who became progenitors of other races.

Between verses 19 and 20 a considerable period of time elapsed, perhaps decades. Ham's youngest son, Canaan, was already born and probably was a young man. Noah had become a farmer, clear evidence that mankind possessed at least a Neolithic culture right after the Flood, and that no long evolutionary process was neces-sary to arrive at such a stage of development. As a farmer he planted a vineyard, made wine, drank too much of it, and became completely drunk. In his drunken stupor, filled with alcohol and evidently very warm, "he uncovered himself"; he threw back his cloak as he lay in his tent and was stark naked. It is hard to be-lieve that Noah was the first farmer to plant grapes and that he was ignorant of the effects of wine. Presumably drunken revelry was one of the sins that had brought on the Flood.

The details of Noah's shame are not presented in this passage; probably there was more to it than merely throwing off his cloak, which served as a sheet or blanket. Scripture does not dwell on Noah's sin but simply presents him as a victim of his immoderation. A giant of the faith who could stand against all the opposition of his generation, he had fallen prey to personal temptation. Scrip-ture never glosses over the faults of such stalwarts, but neither does it expand on details of the seamy side of life.

In what happened next, Canaan, Ham's youngest son, must have had a part. Perhaps he had been the first one to discover his drunken grandfather, and possibly he had made great sport of the whole business as he ran to tell his father about it. Whether Canaan or Ham first saw Noah in his drunken state, Ham "gazed with satisfaction" on Noah according to Leupold's translation,[1] and then went off to tell his brothers about it "with delight."[2] Evi-dently the salutary effects of the Flood already were beginning to lose their grip on Ham. The response of Shem and Japheth to the sin of Noah was just the opposite to that of Ham. They took a robe, and walking into their father's tent backward, covered his nakedness. Certainly it would not have been an evil thing for those men to have seen their father naked, but probably they had no desire to see him in his weakness and have him humiliated in their presence. Very likely Ham saw his brothers perform this act of mercy and was rebuked by it.

When Noah awoke from his drunken stupor, evidently he sensed from the cloak covering him or from some other means that something had happened. Upon inquiry he learned what Ham had done, described in verse 24 of the most versions as his "youngest son." But the text may be translated "younger son" and Ham thus could have been the second son, as the order Shem, Ham, and Japheth indicates. Noah's response was a cursing and blessing on the participants, an event that provided something of a prophetic schema for the races.

"Cursed be Canaan! Servant of servants will he be to his brothers." Clearly the curse was not on Ham but on his youngest son Canaan. The curse does not relegate all the Hamitic peoples to a condition of slavery. Nor does it say they were to be biologically or intellectually inferior to other races. What pro-slavery forces and racists the world over had made of this curse is totally unrelated to the facts. Canaanites lived in Palestine, the land of Canaan, and Phoenicia. They were not a black people, and they have disappeared from history; so obviously the curse, whatever it was, has been completely fulfilled and we have no right to apply it to any modern people. At the time of the Conquest and the Judges, Canaanites who were not exterminated did indeed become servants of the Jews or sons of Shem, as verse 26 predicted. Historical and archaeological studies reveal the Canaanites to have been among the most morally degraded peoples in the ancient Near East—given to infant sacrifice and corrupt sex worship. Those seeds of corruption that were germinating in the persons of their progenitors Canaan and Ham came to full fruit in the Canaanites. Perhaps the curse consigned them to a religious and social inferiority. That religious concerns are paramount in the prophecy seems evident from what is said of Shem and Japheth.

Noah next turned to Shem and said: "Blessed be Yahweh, the God of Shem." Yahweh, the Eternal and Unchangeable One, is

Shem's God. God will be blessed through what He would do in and through Shem and the importance of that action for the world. Abraham was to come from Shem's line and was to head God's special people Israel. And in the fullness of time Christ was to come from that line and to bring blessing to the whole world (Gal. 4:4).

Finally Noah turned to Japheth, the other respectful brother. God would "enlarge" or grant abundant territory to Japheth (whose name means "enlargement"; thus we have a play on words). Japheth's descendants have indeed come to occupy much of the earth's area. That Japheth would "dwell in the tents of Shem" means sharing his hospitality and blessings, and in this context must refer especially to Shem's spiritual history. Through Christ, the greater Son of Abraham and David, and His Jewish disciples, Gentiles have come to share abundantly in the gospel and to have enjoyed its benefits during the last two millennia.

Death of Noah (9:28-29). The topical nature of biblical history and its incompleteness are abundantly demonstrated here. For the next three hundred years the historical narrative is a blank. Then the death of Noah at age 950 is recorded as a proper close to the Flood narrative and a proper introduction to subsequent history.

NOTES

1. H. C. Leupold, *Exposition of Genesis,* 2 vols. (Grand Rapids: Baker, 1942), 1:346.
2. Ibid.

5

HISTORICAL DEVELOPMENTS AFTER THE FLOOD

GENESIS 10:1–11:32

The curious reader is now left with numerous questions. How well did Noah's descendants fare? What was the nature of post-diluvian civilization? To what extent were God's dictates followed by the increasing world population? If God was committed not to judge mankind with a flood, what other kinds of judgment might He or did He pronounce? Partial answers to some of these questions come fairly soon; answers to others are delayed for several chapters. Suffice it to say at this point that the purified environment in which mankind found itself after the Flood did no more to prevent the corruption of society than the perfect environment of Eden. Those who pin their hopes on improving society by cleaning up the social and material environment will be greatly disappointed by this fact.

Having concluded his discussion of Noah in chapter 9, the sacred historian next proceeds to account for the repopulation of the earth after the Flood. Chapter 10 tells how the various national groups descended from Noah's three sons, and chapter 11 introduces the origin of languages and the genealogy of Abraham.

The Table of Nations (10:1-32)

Genesis 10 commonly is called the "Table of Nations" because it presents the origin and spread of national groups. Critics used to argue that the table could not be true, but most of the names in the table now have been discovered in written remains from the ancient Near East and the chapter increasingly is regarded as a trustworthy record.

Most of the names occurring here belonged to individuals, but those individuals came to be progenitors of the nations to which they gave their names. The chapter presents the genealogy of

Noah's sons in the reverse order from the way they appeared in earlier chapters. Thus the more numerous Japhethites are listed first, then the Hamites, and finally the Shemites or Semites. The focus gradually narrows and falls on the line of Shem, from whom Abraham and the other patriarchs descended. The Japhethites spread into Europe and Asia Minor; the Hamites found a home chiefly in Africa; and the Shemites filled southwestern Asia.

The Japhethites (10:1-5). Though there is now considerable agreement in identifying the tribal groups mentioned in this chapter, dogmatism should be avoided. Gomer commonly is identified with the Cimmerians, who migrated from north of the Caucasus and finally settled in Asia Minor (modern Turkey). There is less certainty about Magog. The fact that he seems to be associated with Gomer (Ezek. 38:6) and the way Magog is referred to in a Babylonian text, leads to the conclusion that this tribe is to be placed near the Black Sea and perhaps north of it. Madai is almost unanimously identified with the Medes who lived in ancient times in the mountains south and west of the Caspian Sea. Javan is equated with Ionia, the eastern coast of the Aegean Sea (modern western Turkey). Assyrian inscriptions refer to Tubal and Meshech as peoples living in eastern Asia Minor, northeast of Cilicia. Evidently they were divisions within Magog (Ezek. 38:2). Tiras seems not to refer to Tyre, but beyond that not much can be said positively.

In verses 3 and 4 descendants of Gomer and Javan are singled out as progenitors of tribal groups. Ashkenaz is probably to be identified with the Ashkuz of Assyrian texts, known in English as Scythians and located in the region of Ararat. Riphath apparently lived in north central Asia Minor, while Togarmah has been equated with the Hittite Tegarma, who lived in the vicinity of Carchemish in Syria. Elishah commonly is thought to be Cyprus and Kittim (Kition, modern Larnaka) its capital (cf. Isa. 23:1, 12). Tarshish has been located at Tartessus in southern Spain, on Sardinia, and at various places in the eastern Mediterranean; perhaps the Spanish location has received widest support. Dodanim appears in 1 Chronicles 1:7 as Rodanim; and it is thought that the reading is correct there, the Hebrew *d* and *r* being easy to confuse. If Rodanim is the right reading, Rhodes and its general vicinity must be intended; and that is the usual conclusion among the commentators. Verse 5 seems to imply that the events of 11:1-9 took place before some of the events of chapter 10 occurred (cf. 10:25).

The Hamites (10:6-20). Clearly, the Hamitic peoples were more closely involved with the Hebrews than were the Japhethites. Though most of the Hamites lived in Africa, a significant group spilled over into Canaan, where the Hebrews later contested with them for the mastery. And during the long period of the bondage in Egypt, Israelites found themselves enslaved to other descendants of Ham. The Japhethites were almost completely peripheral to Hebrew experience, however. In this section four primary Hamitic peoples are named (v. 6), and branches of three of them are traced: Cush (vv. 7-12), Mizraim (vv. 13-14), and Canaan (vv. 15-19). The fourth, Phut (Put), may refer to either Libya (Puta) or the land of Punt.

The Cushites (10:7-12). Cush (Kush) for a long time has been associated by scholars with Ethiopia and the Sudan, a country known to the Egyptians as Kush. Scripture also seems to make this identification (Ezek. 30:4; cf. Isa. 11:11 and 45:14). But the Bible also associates Cush with western Asia: with Arabia (1 Chron. 1:9) and with Mesopotamia (Gen. 10:8-12). Babylon, Erech, Akkad, Nineveh and Calah (vv. 10-12) clearly are Mesopotamian sites. Unger concludes that southern Mesopotamia was the original home of the Hamitic Cushites and that they spread from there to Arabia and across the Red Sea into Ethiopia.[1] Stigers believes that the Kishites of Mesopotamia were intended in this passage instead of Ethiopia.[2] Under the circumstances it is unwise to take a dogmatic position, but Unger's argument has considerable merit.

Nimrod (a descendant of Cush) is singled out as "a mighty one" (v. 8, KJV), "a mighty warrior" (NIV), or "the first tyrant,"[3] and as "a mighty hunter" (v. 9). Evidently he was a man of great physical prowess who could exert his will over other men and who built a significant kingdom in lower Mesopotamia. "Mighty hunter" in the context may refer not so much to Nimrod's power over animals as over men.

Mizraim (10:13-14). Mizraim is the Hebrew word for Egypt. A noun with a dual ending, it reflects the fact that Egypt consisted of the "two lands," Upper (southern) and Lower (northern) Egypt in ancient times. The Pathrusim lived in Pathros or Upper Egypt. Caphtor, home of the Caphtorim, is almost unanimously identified as the island of Crete. Jeremiah 47:4 and Amos 9:7 indicate that the Philistines came from Caphtor, which helps to clarify verse 14. Prior to the Hebrew conquest of Canaan, a contingent of Philistines had invaded the area and had liquidated the Avvim or Avvites and occupied their land (Deut. 2:23). That was long before the twelfth-century invasion of Philistines, which threatened the very existence of the Egyptian Empire in the days of Rameses III and then washed onto the shores of Canaan. Evidently, then, the Philistines had a long history of migration (see further discussion of the Philistines under Gen. 21:22-34). The other peoples mentioned in those two verses cannot be identified with any degree of certainty.

The Canaanites (10:15-20). Clearly, the earliest settlers in Canaan were non-Semitic, and there is more detail about the area they occupied than for any other tribal groups. Sidon was early and for a long time dominant among the Phoenician city-states. Heth was the ancestor of the Hittites, who built a kingdom and an empire in Asia Minor during the second millennium B.C., but also had some holdings in Canaan (e.g., Gen. 23:3-20 describes purchase of land from the sons of Heth). The Jebusites lived in and around Jerusalem and held the place until David made it the capital of a united Israel (2 Sam. 5:6-9). The Amorites occupied the hill country of Judea at the time of the Hebrew conquest of Canaan (Josh. 10:5) but were a much more significant Near Eastern people during the second millennium B.C. than such an observation would indicate. For example, Hammurabi, who built the old Babylonian Empire, was the best-known member of the Amorite dynasty that ruled Babylon from 1830 to 1550 B.C. Arka (about eighty miles north of Sidon), Arvad (twenty-five miles north of Arka), Simura (Zemarites, six miles south of Arvad), and Sin (north Phoenician coastal town) were all towns of Phoenicia; and Hamath (modern Hama) stood in the Orontes Valley of Syria.

It is disturbing to many that the peoples who inhabited Canaan are classified as Hamites in Scripture, whereas by the time they appeared significantly on the stage of history during the second millennium B.C. they were clearly Semitic, in language at least. That fact presents no real problem, because language is not necessarily an indication of nationality. Evidently by 2000 B.C. Semites had so extensively infiltrated the area of Canaan that they had reshaped elements of the culture of the area in their own image. That intermixture also had affected Sheba in southwest Arabia, so the people there could be described as descended from Ham (v. 7) and Shem (v. 28). Likewise, descendants of Cush are said to have settled in Mesopotamia at an early date (as noted above), although during much of ancient history Semites were in control there. Thus, as is clear from verse 22, the peoples there also were descended from Shem. It is also interesting to observe that the Hittites are said to have descended from Ham, but the Hittites of the Hittite kingdom and empire periods were Indo-Europeans. Actually what happened is that Indo-European Japhethites invaded Asia Minor shortly after 2000 B.C. and became the ruling element in the new Hittite society, dominating the populace that was already settled in the area.

As a generalization, it seems that after the Flood the Japhethites spread from the region of Ararat in a northwesterly and southwesterly direction around the Black Sea. Hamites moved south into Mesopotamia and southwestward into eastern Asia Minor, through Canaan and into Africa. Semites expanded southward into Arabia and gradually infiltrated Mesopotamia and Canaan, so that those areas became known as Semitic. Moreover, they also came to dominate Sheba (as noted) and eventually crossed over to Africa, entering Ethiopia and establishing a line there that claimed to be descended from Solomon. That dynasty terminated when Haile Selassie was dethroned in 1974.

The Shemites (Semites) (10:21-32). Attention now turns to Shem and his descendants and continues to focus on them through the remainder of Genesis. These people more commonly are called Semites, the spelling "Sem" coming through the Greek. Semites are divided linguistically into Northwest Semitic (Aramaic, Phoenician, Ugaritic, Canaanite: Hebrew, Moabite), South Semitic (Arabic and Ethiopic), and East Semitic (Akkadian: Babylonian and Assyrian).

Immediately in verse 21 we are informed that for the writer the most important branch of the Semites were the "sons of Eber," which of course included "Abram the Hebrew" (Gen. 14:13). "Eber" provides the apparent source of the word *Hebrew* and comes from the verb meaning "to pass over." There are two major branches of the family of Eber: Joktan and Peleg. The first is delineated here and the second is reserved for chapter 11, where it introduces the family and biography of Abraham.

Most of the places mentioned in 10:21-32 are hard to locate specifically, but they must be placed in the general vicinity of Arabia or nearby lands. Elam was, of course, just east of Mesopotamia; its capital was at Susa (biblical Shushan), stage for the drama of Esther and launching point for the activities of Nehemiah. Asshur was northern Mesopotamia, and Arphaxad is thought by some to have been northeast of Nineveh. Aram had as its center Damascus in Syria, and Haran is the adjacent region of northwestern Mesopotamia. Lud is identified as Lydia in western Asia Minor, where an Assyrian merchant colony was established by 2000 B.C. Sheba was a kingdom of southwest Arabia known for its perfumes, gold, and precious stones. Ophir, also a source of gold but not yet located, is thought to have lain along the coast of east Africa.

The Tower of Babel (11:1-9)

The Flood had eradicated multitudes of sinful people but not the sin nature. No one knows how much time had elapsed since the Flood, but its effects evidently had lost their impact. In an effort to glorify and fortify themselves and to prevent the will of God from being fulfilled in the dispersion of the races, the peoples of earth launched construction of a massive tower in lower Mesopotamia.

At that time "all the inhabitants of the earth had one language and one vocabulary." The Hebrew seems to indicate that various dialects had not yet appeared. Under such conditions, communication among peoples was swift, and plans for a building project were easily propagated. As the population spread "eastward," southeastward from the Ararat region, they reached a "plain in Shinar" (Babylonia) and "settled down there." At length they decided to launch a massive building project and excitedly exhorted one another, "Come on, let us make bricks. . . . Come on, let us build." Lacking stone and timber in a region of waterlaid soil, they used clay brick for construction; and the extensive bitumen deposits of the Mesopotamian Valley provided mortar. In pride they sought to build a city and tower as a rallying point and as a symbol of or memorial to *their* greatness. Genesis does not say that they intended to enter heaven by means of this tower or that they planned to use it for worship purposes. The Hebrew simply calls it a *migdal* ("tower"), which could be used for defense or in a number of other ways. It is doubtful, therefore, whether this tower could have had any connection with the ziggurates or stage towers of ancient Mesopotamia, constructed for worship and crowned with a temple on the topmost level. (It is commonly held in liberal theological circles that the ziggurat at Babylon or nearby Birs Nimrud figured in a late myth composed to account for the origin of languages.) Moreover, ziggurates evolved in Mesopotamia during the third millennium B.C., long after the appearance of languages and dialects in the region.

The sin of the builders was at least twofold. In their pride they wanted to make for themselves a name. Thus they spared no effort to erect a structure so colossal that it would bring great glory to themselves. But their major concern was that they might have a rallying point in order to avoid being "scattered over the face of the whole earth" (v. 4, NIV). In direct disobedience to God's specific command to "be fruitful and multiply, and fill the earth" (Gen. 9:1), they tried to avoid being scattered abroad. And they sought a cohesive element of their own making, instead of rallying around a divinely appointed magnet. Those builders discovered that with their inner oneness of spiritual purpose gone, they had to provide an element of social cement of their own concoction. Stigers concludes that in making a name for themselves, they also sought to create a worldwide imperialistic power, which would facilitate the advance of evil designs as the influence for good declined on the earth.[4]

"And God came down" is another way of saying, "God intervened." Instead of allowing things to take their course as He usually does, He now interfered in judgment to stop what men "were building." With apprehension, He observed, "This is only the beginning of what they will do." If they succeeded in that venture, they would be encouraged to try almost anything. Their efforts would result in a high degree of success because of their unity of language, their facility of communication. So the obvious practical course of action was to create barriers to communication, to disrupt their ability to continue unified activity. God determined to "confuse their language" in order to prevent further con-

struction. Unable to communicate, they drifted off in little groups
to all points of the compass and thus achieved the filling of the
earth that God originally had ordered. Evidently that judgment
took place before the scattering reported in chapter 10 could have
taken place (cf. 10:5, 32). As people scattered, work on the tower
and city were no longer feasible. The repeated use of Yahweh in
the Hebrew of this passage underscores God's mercy and redemption. In confusing their language and in scattering them, God pre-
vented men from devising greater corporate mischief and thus
injuring themselves further. "Let *us* go down" indicates plurality
in the Godhead and helps to support the concept of trinity.

"Wherefore its name is called Babel because there Yahweh
made a babble of the languages of all the earth."[5] Babel means
"gate of God," but here is a play on a word. "Confuse" is from the
verb *bālal*, a form of which (*balbel*) is contracted to Babel. God
called the place where He executed judgment Babel because there
He confused the language or made a babble. "Babylon" is a translation of the same Hebrew word as "Babel." A major step on humanity's way back from that confusion occurred at Pentecost in
the preaching of one gospel in such a way that it could be understood by those speaking many languages. The final reversal is
predicted in Zephaniah 3:9: "Yea, at that time I will change the
speech of the peoples to a pure speech, that all of them may call
on the name of the LORD and serve him with one accord" (RSV).[6]
Babylon came to symbolize godlessness and godless society in
Scripture, and in Revelation characterizes the ultimate in moral
corruption (Rev. 18:1-5).

The Ancestry of Abraham (11:10-32)

As the clans of earth went their separate ways and as they
strayed ever farther from God, He sought a people of His own that
would be an effective witness to His name in the world. Quickly
the sacred historian rushed across the centuries with his genealogical account until he came to rest on the family of Abraham, from
which the Messiah ultimately was to arise.

The arrangement of the genealogy presumably is schematic.
Ten generations appear, the same as in chapter 5. Apparently the
Hebrews liked balanced divisions in genealogies (cf. the three
equal lists of fourteen genealogies each in Matt. 1:17). We know

that the lists of Matthew are not complete, and indications are
that the lists of Genesis 5 and 11 are not either. The information
given in this chapter includes the age of a predecessor when each
person was born and the length of that predecessor's life. A comparison of this genealogy with that of chapter 5 reveals that both
the lifespan and the age of paternity were gradually dropping.
And in this chapter there is no mention of death as in chapter 5.
Here God's purpose is not to emphasize the effects of sin but to
concentrate instead on the forward march of humanity toward the
coming of the Redeemer.

At length the genealogical listing comes to Terah, the father of
Abram. It is not necessary to conclude that at age seventy Terah
begat triplets—Abram, Nahor, and Haran—but that at seventy he
fathered one of them and the others came in due course. Presumably all three of those sons are mentioned because they figure significantly in subsequent history. Nahor was the father of Bethuel,
and Bethuel the father of Rebekah, beloved wife of Jacob. Haran
was, of course, the father of Lot, who is at the center of much of
the narrative to follow.

The family home of Terah, and thus Abram, was Ur of the
Chaldees. That city has been located by some in northern Mesopotamia in recent years, but the idea has not found widespread
support; the traditional identification of this site with the Ur north
of the Persian Gulf seems preferable. At its height about 2000
B.C., Ur probably would have been the greatest city in the world
during at least part of Abram's lifespan. Anywhere he might have
followed God by faith would have taken him to a lesser home.
While the clan was still in Ur, Haran died and Lot was fatherless.
That is the first recorded instance of a son preceding his father in
death, except for the murder of Abel. And while still in Ur, Abram
had married Sarai, his half-sister, and she remained barren for
many years to come.

Verse 31 might almost seem to imply that God appeared to
Terah and called him to leave Ur, but such apparently was not the
case. God appeared to Abram while in Ur and called him to leave
his land and kindred and go to a land He would show him (Acts
7:2-4). That revelation could have coincided with Terah's decision to lead the clan to Haran, no matter what reason he chose
to do so. As an obedient son, Abram followed the patriarch and

remained with Terah in Haran until he died. For the moment
Abram had followed what light he had; after his father's death
God again would command him to get moving to a land of God's
revelation (Gen. 12:1). There is no indication that Abram was
disobedient to God in going only to Haran with his father or that
God was displeased with him for incomplete obedience. He did
not know where God's promised land was. It was Moses' comment
that Haran was the first stop on the way to Canaan (Gen. 11:31).
Evidently Terah and other members of Abram's clan were idola-
ters in Ur (Josh. 24:2), a city especially devoted to the worship
of the moon god. Haran was also a center of moon worship, and
for that reason Terah may have chosen to stay there.

Terah's age of 205 years at death (v. 32) presents a difficulty,
assuming that Abram had been born when his father was seventy
(v. 26). That would make Abram 135 at the time of his father's
death, though Genesis 12:4 states he was 75. The problem may
be solved by concluding that Abram was Terah's youngest son and
that he was listed in verse 26 because of his prominence. An alter-
nate solution is found in the Samaritan text of Genesis, which says
Terah was 145 at death.

NOTES

1. Merrill F. Unger, *Archeology and the Old Testament* (Grand Rapids:
   Zondervan, 1954), p. 83.
2. Harold G. Stigers, *A Commentary on Genesis* (Grand Rapids: Zondervan,
   1976), p. 124.
3. Ibid.
4. Ibid., p. 129.
5. H. C. Leupold, *Exposition of Genesis,* 2 vols. (Grand Rapids: Baker,
   1942), 1:390-91.
6. Derek Kidner, *Genesis* (Downers Grove, Ill.: Inter-Varsity, 1967), p. 110.

6

ABRAHAM (1)
COVENANT AND EARLY YEARS IN CANAAN

GENESIS 12:1–17:27

Abraham (Abram) was one of the most significant figures in all of Scripture, and for that matter, in all of history. He was the father of the Israelites through Isaac, the son of promise, and father of the Arabs through Ishmael. He was the ancestor of the Messiah (Matt. 1:1) and the spiritual father of all who share in his faith by the Holy Spirit (Rom. 4:11-12). His exercise of faith in answering God's call to leave his home and in offering his son Isaac furnishes outstanding examples of faith for believers of all ages (Heb. 11:8-19). And God's covenant with Abraham provides a basis for the preservation of the Jew, the millennial hope, and the ordering of world affairs at the end of the age.

First Covenant Announcement and Initial Obedience (12:1-9)

Presumably verse 1 records God's second appearance to Abram to call him from among his relatives and his pagan society. The first call had come at Ur, this one at Haran after the death of Terah. This time God begins to announce provisions of the Abrahamic Covenant. These are first personal: "I will bless you"; "I will make your name great"; "you will be a blessing." The blessing on him may be construed as involving an heir, spiritual enjoyment, and material provision. His name would be glorified by being known as father of the faithful and the father of a new race of people. Abram's blessing to others would occur in his own day as he acted as preservative salt (e.g., rescuing the people of the plain, Gen. 14; Lot, Gen. 19) and would extend to subsequent generations through Christ or other outstanding descendants. The provisions of the covenant also specifically related to his descendants. He was to be the father of "a great nation." But the covenant went beyond his posterity to include "all families of the earth." That could be fulfilled only through the ministry of Christ and the Scriptures (produced by his descendants).

Further, God announced that treatment of Abram's descendants would be a basis for blessing or judging the nations (v. 3). Again and again this principle is operative in the prophets as they pronounce judgment on the nations surrounding Israel for the treatment of His chosen people.

The requirements of Abram's call and covenant were faith and obedience: faith to believe that God would do as He promised and obedience to the command to leave his home and kindred and go to a land of God's choosing as evidence of his faith. He fully met the requirements (Heb. 11:8).

Presumably without undue delay Abram obeyed, striking out at age seventy-five with his wife, his nephew Lot, and some servants and belongings. Evidently he did not yet know where the promised land was but had some promptings to go in the direction of Canaan. The route probably took him through Damascus (cf. Gen. 15:2-3) and then south to Shechem. There, between Mount Ebal and Mount Gerizim (about thirty miles north of Jerusalem), God again appeared to Abram and pronounced yet another aspect of the covenant: He would some day give Canaan to Abram's descendants. Abram was not yet strong enough to expel the Canaanites and take their lands. Nor had the moral conditions of the Canaanites become so vile as to warrant God's command to the Hebrews to exterminate them, as was true at the time of the conquest. In gratitude Abram built an altar for thanksgiving and worship.

Shechem became an important center to the Israelites. In Joshua's day all Israel met there to rehearse the blessings of the Law (Deut. 11:29) and later to hear Joshua's farewell address (Josh. 24:2-28). When Rehoboam sought to head off the revolt that split the kingdom, he met with leaders of the people at Shechem—to no avail (1 Kings 12:1). Long centuries after the area had become a stronghold for Samaritan worship, Jesus dignified it with His presence and ministry (John 4).

Subsequently Abram moved farther south to Bethel (about ten miles north of Jerusalem) and in its vicinity built a second altar.

Then he continued on his journey southward to the Negev and thus traversed the entire land from north to south. Perhaps in some sense he was engaged in a reconnaissance mission.

Sojourn in Egypt (12:10-20)   *Test of Truest*

Not long after Abram entered Canaan, a severe famine hit the area. Whether or not it was especially sent or permitted by God, it did prove to be a test of the patriarch's faith. Evidently Abram failed the test and sought his own solution to his problem. When the dry farming of Palestine was unable to produce adequate food supplies, he turned to the irrigation farming of Egypt to meet his needs.

Going to Egypt for help was not in itself a sinful act, any more than it was for Israel in the days of Joseph, or for the holy family after the birth of Christ. Abram's failure lay in his neglect to call on God for sustenance or marching orders. Moreover, his sin was compounded by deception. Fearing for his life, he represented his wife as his sister. In reality she was his half sister (Gen. 20: 12); and that misrepresentation was part of a preconceived plan adopted probably soon after leaving Haran (Gen. 20:13). That the duplicity was mutually advantageous is evident, for the death of Abram would have left Sarai without any protection in a strange land. At this time Abram was about seventy-five (12:4) and Sarai some ten years younger (Gen. 17:17). Evidently for the patriarchs, not only the lifespan was lengthened but life processes were also spread out over a longer period of time. At about sixty-five Sarai still appeared to be a young woman of child-bearing age.

It turned out as Abram had feared. Sarai's beauty was noised abroad and she wound up in Pharaoh's harem. The expected gifts were presented to the woman's guardian, in this case her "brother." Now God must step in because if Sarai were lost to Abram, the Abrahamic Covenant, the rise of the Hebrew nation as a witness to God in the world, and the arrangements for the coming of the Messiah would all be endangered. Through plagues imposed on Pharaoh and his household, God somehow informed Pharaoh of Abram and Sarai's true relationship.

Pharaoh administered a stern rebuke to Abram and forcibly ejected him from the country; thus he returned to the land of promise, which evidently he should never have left in the first place. Abram stood silent before the condemnation of Pharaoh. How sad it is when unbelievers evidence greater integrity than believers and have to sit in judgment on them for their failures! God never varnishes over the faults of the "heroes of faith," and that is sometimes noted as an evidence for inspiration. If the Scriptures were merely of human origin, presumably the author would seek to cover some of these flaws in order to make a good story.

Separation from Lot (13:1-18)   *Test of Values*

Expelled from Egypt, Abram returned to Canaan by way of the "Negev." The Negev is a great triangle of land with its apex on the Gulf of Aqaba (an arm of the Red Sea) and its base on a line extending east and west and running south of Beersheba. Explorations have shown that numerous settlements dotted the Negev between about 2000 and 1800 B.C. but did not exist for long periods of time before and after those dates. Such settlements made possible the journey of people and flocks and herds through an arid region and help to date the patriarchal period. Abraham, Jacob, and Joseph and the caravan that sold him into slavery in Egypt, all needed a line of settlements to facilitate their journey through this inhospitable area. If one accepts without question reckonings based on the Hebrew text, one can develop a rather firm date for Abram. Of course it is necessary to work backward. Solomon began to reign about 970 B.C. It is stated in 1 Kings 6:1 that the Exodus took place 480 years before the fourth year of Solomon's reign, or about 1446. Exodus 12:40-41 puts the entrance of the patriarchs into Egypt 430 years earlier—about 1876. From a study of Genesis 12:4; 21:5; 25:26; and 47:9 it is inferred that the patriarchs sojourned in Canaan 215 years, entering about 2091. In these references it is clear that Abram entered Canaan at 75, Isaac was born to him at 100, Isaac was 60 at Jacob's birth, and Jacob was 130 when he stood before Pharaoh. A total of 215 years elapsed, then, between Abram's entrance into Canaan and Jacob's entrance into Egypt. If Abram was 75 when he entered Canaan, his birth would have occurred in about 2166 B.C.

Abram's wealth is measured not merely in kind ("livestock") but in bullion ("silver and gold"). Abram's possession and use of precious metals has led Cyrus Gordon and others to conclude that

Abram was a merchant prince;[1] see also such passages as Genesis
23:16, with its reference to "current money with the merchant."

As Abram journeyed northward, at length he came to the vicinity of Bethel, where he had first erected an altar for worship
after his entrance into Canaan. There he "called on the name of
the Lord," probably meaning that he restored his fellowship with
God. He returned to the life of dependence on God by faith.

Lot had traveled from Mesopotamia to Canaan with Abram.
Evidently he also had accompanied his uncle to Egypt but played
no important part in events there. Now he appears on center
stage again. The flocks and herds of Abram and Lot had multi-
plied rapidly, and there were not enough pasture lands and water
holes to provide for all of them if they stayed together. Earlier
the land supplied inadequate resources because of famine; now it
"could not support them" because of increase in livestock. So a
new test of faith had arisen for Abram. Conflicts over meager resources grew more frequent between the herdsmen of Abram and
Lot. The problem was compounded by the fact that Canaanites
and Perizzites also shared the land with them. The latter may
have been only one of the tribes of Canaanites in Palestine rather
than a separate ethnic group.

Having renewed his faith near Bethel, Abram was now better
prepared to handle the pressing problems of life. In dealing with
Lot, he demonstrated wisdom, generosity, and insight. Wisely he
determined that the best way to overcome the lack of resources
was for him and Lot to separate. Generously he offered Lot his
choice of the best lands of Palestine, refusing to assert his own
rights and trusting God to meet his needs. Evidencing great insight, perhaps spiritual insight, he recognized that they could not
afford to engage in quarrels before a pagan world: "for we are
brothers."

When Lot "scanned the whole plain of the Jordan," he saw that
it was "well irrigated," "like the land of Egypt." It was green and
productive as far south as Zoar in those early days (13:10; cf.
19:22). Such luxuriant conditions would have been quite alien to
the thinking of readers in Moses' day or later because by then
God's judgment on Sodom and Gomorrah had reduced the southern part of that region to a sterile, burned out condition. Informa-

tion of this sort helps to build a case against the assertion of critics that Genesis is a compilation of sources originating in Palestine during the first millennium B.C. Such writers would not know the earlier condition of the region.

Lot chose an area that would bring monetary advantage, without consideration of its ultimate effects on him. He simply would not be able to stand against the unbridled wickedness of Sodom. The course of Lot's spiritual descent began when he "pitched his tents near Sodom" (v. 12, NIV) and continued as he moved into town and settled in a house there, and as he became one of the elders or leaders of the city and sat in the place of leadership—"the city gate" (Gen. 19:1). Those stages of decline are reminiscent of Psalm 1:1: "Blessed is the man who does not *walk* in the counsel of the wicked or *stand* in the way of sinners or *sit* in the seat of mockers" (NIV, italics added). Though tainted by the sin of his environment, Lot never quite capitulated to it; he was "distressed by the filthy lives of lawless men" and "tormented . . . by the lawless deeds he saw and heard" (2 Pet. 2:7-8 NIV).

Abram stayed in the land of Canaan, in the highlands, where water and food were a little less plentiful than in the plain of the Jordan but where people were fewer and opportunities for expansion greater. After looking at the fruitful lands of the Jordan Valley, Lot had made a decision based on sight. By faith Abram had made a decision to follow God in Canaan, and now he was rewarded by sight. God told him to lift up his eyes and look about him. In further confirmation and elaboration of the Abrahamic Covenant, God promised to Abram this land of Canaan in perpetuity: to him and his descendants "forever." And that promise applied not only to land as far as he could see but also to all the "length and breadth of the land" where he should wander. Moreover, his offspring now were declared to be innumerable.

Then Abram "acquired grazing rights"[2] in the area of the oaks of Mamre (named for an Amorite, Gen. 14:13) near Hebron. Hebron is nineteen miles southwest of Jerusalem on the road to Beersheba and the traditional site of Mamre a little over a mile north of Hebron. At Mamre today one may see a well-constructed enclosure wall erected by the Emperor Hadrian in the second century A.D. Inside is a "well of Abraham" and the ruins of a church built by Constantine over Hadrian's pagan shrine. And Hadrian's shrine is supposed to have been built on the site of Abram's altar in a deliberate effort to desecrate that holy place.

Deliverance of Lot (14:1-24)   *Test of Love & Loyalty*

Just as the wealth of the plain of the Jordan had attracted Lot, so it had attracted foreign invaders. A coalition of four eastern kings had conquered Syria, Transjordan, and the plain of the Jordan. After thirteen years of foreign domination, those subjugated peoples had risen against their conquerors and struck for freedom. The eastern kings then launched a fierce punitive expedition that thoroughly squashed the peoples of Transjordan. When the invaders reached the plain of the Jordan, the kings of the five cities (Sodom et al.) located there determined to make a stand against them but also were soundly defeated. The record of the event might never have been preserved were it not for the fact that Lot and his family and possessions were carried off in the general looting following the defeat.

Critics used to doubt the historical validity of this account on the grounds that the names of the Mesopotamian kings were fictitious; there was no such extensive travel from Mesopotamia to Palestine in the days of Abraham; and there was no such route of march through Transjordan. All that is changed now. The names of the kings have proved to be linguistically identifiable, though not yet connected with specific rulers. Evidences of such travel have been found, and the route of conquest (later called "The King's Way," Num. 20:17; 21:22) has a continuous history of use from the third millennium B.C. to the present. In fact, today one may motor in comfort on a blacktop highway that follows that route. Moreover, archaeological and historical evidence shows that about 2000-1900 B.C. the civilization of Transjordan was so thoroughly wiped out that it did not recover for centuries. It is tempting to identify that massive destruction with the punitive expedition of Genesis 14.

The Vale of Siddim, where the king of Sodom and his compatriots took their stand, was by Moses' day "the salt sea" (v. 3). Evidently, during the several centuries between Abraham and Moses, the Dead Sea gradually rose and covered much of the Vale of Siddim, submerging Sodom and the other cities that formerly

had stood there. The common view today is that they once occupied land where the shallow southern basin of the Dead Sea
now lies.

When the word of the defeat and of Lot's capture reached
Abram "the Hebrew" (first time the term is used) at Mamre, he
immediately launched an expeditionary force. He could command
"318 trained men born in his household," evidently retained to
protect his considerable holdings. And he was confederate with
three local chiefs—Aner, Eshcol, and Mamre—who may have had
bands of men who served as mercenaries, or at least would jump
at the chance to seize booty. How many men Abram commanded
must be left open to conjecture. They quickly covered the some
120 miles from Mamre to Dan, where they intercepted the foe.
To walk that distance would have exhausted them; mules could
not have carried them northward rapidly. It has been suggested
that they sped in hot pursuit by camel. At any rate, they conducted
a surprise attack at night in a rear guard action, dividing their
forces into more than one company (v. 15) to give the appearance
of greater numbers than they actually possessed. Presumably they
also enjoyed divine help. After the attack they pursued the fleeing
eastern forces all the way to Hobah north of Damascus, making
sure they could not regroup and return south. Then they circled
back and collected the booty and prisoners and returned to Sodom.
How long the entire operation took we are left to guess.

The fact that Abram had 318 trained men in his entourage gives
some hint regarding the size of the patriarchal establishment. If
those men were married (as would have been likely if they were
in continuous employ or servitude) and had only one child each
on the average, Abram as patriarch would have ruled and led in
worship a community of a thousand or more. Such a company
would have given him considerable power and prestige and personal safety, but would have created numerous problems of
supply.

As Abram came south after the defeat of the four kings of the
east, he met two important personages: the king of Sodom and the
king of Salem. At least the former met him in the Valley of Shaveh
or the King's Valley. Evidently that was near Jerusalem; most
identify it as the Kidron on the east, but some as the Hinnon on
the west and south of the city. Probably the news of Abram's vic-

tory traveled south quickly, and the king of Sodom had gone north to meet the conqueror and express his gratitude, and to strike a bargain with him in order to regain his people and goods.

Probably even before Abram and the king of Sodom met, Melchizedek (meaning "king of righteousness"), king of Salem (a shortened form of "Jerusalem"), hailed the conqueror. After presenting "bread and wine," needed rations for hungry and thirsty troops, he bestowed a blessing on Abram. As a "king" of Jerusalem and "priest" of the "God Most High," whom Abram worshiped, Melchizedek was in that blessing demonstrating friendship and perhaps spiritual kinship. Whether he was a remnant left on earth of the original true monotheism or a recipient of special revelation as Abram must be left open to question. At any rate, he recognized Abram's victory as a result of divine intervention. Accepting the truth of that pronouncement, Abram concluded that therefore all the spoils of war belonged to God. In recognition of that fact, he gave a tenth or a tithe of the spoils to Melchizedek.

Evidently as the spoils were being assessed and divided out, the king of Sodom entered the picture. Perhaps fearful that the conqueror might keep the captives as slaves or sell them into slavery, the king of Sodom offered all the spoils to Abram if he would release the people. Abram's response was clear, "I have raised my hand," or sworn to God, "that I will accept nothing belonging to you." In effect he was not going to manipulate control of the promised land himself but was going to trust God, who evidently was in control of things. He would not use the spoils to his own advantage, nor would he take advantage of his allies, nor would he ally himself with the people of the plain of the Jordan. He would take nothing for himself or his men; his allies would be given their share; the people of the plain would be free to go home and take their goods with them. That magnanimity and trust in God brought a divine response as described in chapter 15.

But first a further comment on Melchizedek is in order because Hebrews 7 makes extended reference to him. Melchizedek must be viewed as a type of Christ, whose priesthood was of a higher order than Aaron's. The argument in Hebrews seems to be that just as Melchizedek did not exercise his priesthood because of descent in a priestly family but by direct appointment of God, so

Christ did not exercise His priesthood by descent in the priestly line of Levi but on the superior basis of God's direct appointment.

The Covenant Confirmed (15:1-21)

As was clear from Abram's statement to the king of Sodom, he was trusting God completely to bring about fulfillment of His covenant promises. But the years were passing and there was no evidence that God was keeping His word. Especially, Abram did not yet have a son, and Sarai could hardly be expected to have one in advanced age. Often God seems to delay His intervention until a situation becomes absolutely hopeless; then a solution will have to be of His doing and all the glory will be His. Such would be the case with Abram and Sarai as time relentlessly moved on until Sarai reached ninety and then bore a son; and with Jairus' daughter and Lazarus, whose illnesses were allowed to end in death in order that the marvelous power of God could be demonstrated in resurrection (see Luke 8:41-56; John 11:1-46).

In the midst of Abram's consternation, God appeared to him in a "vision." Some commentators try to distinguish between visions, dreams, trances, and the like; but it is best not to get caught up in a discussion of mechanics or technicalities here. The important fact to note is that God was revealing Himself to Abram in a way clearly to be distinguished from any subconscious or heightened personal perceptions. Evidently that was the fifth time God revealed Himself to Abram. The exhortation to "fear not" (v. 1) has been connected by some with a possible retaliation by the eastern kings, but the context indicates that Abram's fear primarily concerned his being childless.

Abram addressed God as "Adonai Yahweh," the first name indicating *master* and the second *covenant keeper*. That rare form of address is beautifully translated in the NIV as "Sovereign Lord." Then Abram asked somewhat plaintively, "What can you give me" or "What could you give me, seeing I am going on bereft of children?" Conditioned by his social milieu, the patriarch assumed that his trusted head servant Eliezer would be his heir if he died childless. The social texts from Nuzi in northern Mesopotamia demonstrate that it was common for childless couples to adopt a servant or some other young man as an heir. Then God categor-

ically declared that his heir would be his own natural son and
asserted that his offspring would be as numerous as the stars of the
heavens. Abram had asked, "What *can you give* me?" God answered in effect, "Natural descendants as numerous as the stars if
you can count them." God could do something that would boggle
Abram's mind.

The patriarch unreservedly trusted God's word of promise; he
"believed Yahweh," the covenant keeper. And God "credited it to
him for righteousness." He implicitly and unequivocally trusted
the "Sovereign Lord" as the one superior to all natural processes
and the one who would do what He promises; and on the basis of
Abram's faith God justified him or declared him righteous. But
this was not Abram's first exercise of profound faith in God; apparently that came when God first called him at Ur (Heb. 11:8-
10). That statement of saving faith is the basis of Paul's great
declaration of justification by faith in Romans 4 and Galatians 3
and demonstrates that salvation comes on the same basis—of
faith—in all ages.

In verse 7 God moved on to the other part of the covenant: the
land to be inherited. Abram seemed to ask in a spirit of reverential
trust: "O Sovereign Lord, how can I know that I will gain possession of it?" (NIV). The divine answer was to instruct the patriarch to make the usual preparations for solemnizing a covenant
(vv. 9-10; cf. Jer. 34:18-20). Normally both parties to a covenant
would pass between the two halves of the animals, but in this case
only God did, showing the one-sided and unconditional nature of
the promises made. Two nights and a day were involved in the
revelation and covenant of chapter 15. God used the stars as an
object lesson on the first night. During the day Abram prepared
the animals as God instructed and chased away the birds of prey.
Then at sunset a "dreadful darkness," the terror of the Lord,
descended on Abram and "a smoking fire pot with a blazing torch"
(v. 17, NIV) passed between the pieces. This evidently was a
theophany or manifestation of God, as were the pillar of fire and
smoke that led the marching throng of Israelites in the wilderness.
The elaboration of God's covenant with Abram on that occasion
contains at least three elements: (1) the boundaries of the promised land; (2) the variety of peoples inhabiting it; and (3) a statement concerning perpetual occupation of it.

The boundaries of the promised land are delineated as the river of Egypt and the river Euphrates (v. 18). The Hebrew word translated "river" of Egypt refers to an ever-flowing river and apparently must be applied to the Nile; other streams of southern Palestine and the Sinai flow only during the rainy season. The easternmost branch of the Nile, the Pelusiac, flows out near modern Port Said and hence near the ancient line of fortifications that protected Egypt from marauding Asiatics. Thus the Pelusiac branch properly could be thought of as the border of Egypt. The distance from Port Said to the Euphrates is some 600 miles, measured in an arc. Of course the Hebrews never have enjoyed possession of all that land; fulfillment of the covenant must be reserved for the millennial day at the end times. The variety of peoples occupying the promised land in Abram's day is tabulated in verses 19-21.

An important provision of the Abrahamic Covenant is that occupation of the land forever (Gen. 13:15) does not mean unbroken occupation from Abram's day forward. It means permanent occupation only after the whole land is taken. In fact, an extended period of exile is forecast here, to be followed by others later. That period of bondage was set at 400 years and was in Egypt, of course. Possibly that period may be viewed as a round number, for Exodus 12:40 gives a more exact 430 years of sojourn in Egypt. Or the time of bondage may have been about 400 years and the total sojourn 430 years, with about thirty years of favorable treatment at the hands of the Egyptians before enslavement. The reference to the fourth generation (Gen. 15:16) could be roughly equivalent to 400 years if one thinks of four patriarchal lifetimes.

The last part of verse 16 is very arresting: "the iniquity of the Amorites is not yet complete." This implies that in the counsels of divine justice a quota of iniquity is allowed a given nation before it is punished in a minor way or by obliteration. And it seems that God will deal with a nation when it has reached such a place. After the period of bondage in Egypt, God gave orders to the Hebrews to destroy the Amorites utterly (Deut. 20:17). Apparently the iniquity of the Amorites was "complete" or "full" by that time.

The Birth of Ishmael (16:1-16)

The years continued to roll on. Abram was now 85 and Sarai 75.

No son had yet been born to fulfill the covenant. Now Sarai urged a solution to the problem, a solution that was widely employed in ancient Western Asia and was even codified in the Code of Hammurabi. When a wife was barren, she could provide her husband with a concubine, commonly a slave, for the purpose of child bearing. The child born was then counted as the child of the wife and enjoyed full legal rights. It is to be remembered that Jacob acquiesced to that arrangement later on and that children born in this way became full family members and heads of some of the twelve tribes of Israel. However common that practice may have been, it was not God's answer to Abram's cry for an heir. The great patriarch fell from the pinnacle of faith on which he had been perched in previous chapters and allowed himself to be guided by circumstances and his wife rather than God. Paul in Galatians 4 compares Hagar's son, "born after the flesh," to self-effort in religion. Abram's course of action proved to be disastrous for all concerned—for Sarai, Hagar, Abram, Isaac, and Ishmael and the peace and harmony of the family.

Hagar's haughty attitude toward Sarai because of her ability to give Abram a child resulted in such severe retaliation that Hagar fled the intolerable conditions. An Egyptian who had come north with Abram some ten years earlier, Hagar now fled toward her homeland. Near the border of Egypt "the angel of the Lord," commonly interpreted to be a preincarnate appearance of Christ, met her with significant assurances. Primarily she was promised numerous descendants in terms reminiscent of God's covenant with Abram. Then she was comforted with the declaration that God had heard her cries of misery and had intervened on her behalf, in testimony of which she was to name her child Ishmael ("God hears"). The observation that Ishmael would be "a wild man" (KJV), better "a wild ass of a man" (RSV), refers to the wild onager that roamed the desert as freedom-loving Bedouins were destined to do in later years. Ishmael was, of course, the ancestor of the Arabs.

The Covenant Reaffirmed (17:1-27)

The years ebbed away, thirteen more of them. God had made magnificent promises to Abram, but fulfillment was not forthcoming. Eliezer of Damascus was not to be his heir, neither was

Ishmael. Abram was now 99 and Sarai about 89; there was no hope of their having children. Into that impossible situation God came with a renewal of the covenant and the pronouncement: "You will be the father of many nations." In celebration of the fact, his name was to be changed from Abram ("exalted father") to Abraham ("father of a multitude"). In His reaffirmation of the covenant, God stressed that it would be "everlasting," that Canaan was to be an "everlasting possession," and that "kings" would arise in his line.

The mention of kings is a foregleam of the Davidic line, for David was in the lineage of Abraham. It is important here to add the Davidic Covenant to the Abrahamic Covenant. In it (2 Sam. 7) God promised to David a line forever, a throne forever, and a kingdom forever. It is clear from the prophetic message of both the Old and New Testaments that the eternal aspects of the Abrahamic and Davidic covenants could be fulfilled only in Christ—the greater son of Abraham and David. He will rule on the throne of David during the millennial period and in the New Jerusalem after the creation of the new heaven and the new earth (Rev. 21).

Although God's covenant with Abraham was perpetual and irrevocable, Abraham was assigned an obligation that served as a sign and seal of the covenant. All males of Abraham's larger family were to be circumcised on the eighth day. That obligation applied to Hebrews, their servants, and slaves, and signified that they were marked off from other people as God's peculiar possession. Though circumcision was practiced widely in the ancient Near East, it was now given a new meaning for the Hebrews: commitment to God's people and to God. Circumcision subsequently brought the infant into covenant relationship with God and could not be confused with the puberty rites of peoples surrounding the Hebrews.

God then proceeded to bring Sarai directly into the covenant and specifically to predict an heir. He changed the form of her name to Sarah, meaning "princess," and announced that she would be "the mother of nations." The promise of numerous descendants was not merely to Abraham and to be fulfilled through a secondary wife; it was to be fulfilled through Abraham *and* Sarah. Abraham fell on his face in wonder and adoration, but at the same time laughed incredulously. He had mixed emotions, demonstrating doubt and faith. Then, in effect, Abraham asked two questions:

"Will Sarah and I indeed have a son? What about my beloved
Ishmael; will you also bless him?" To the first God responded with
an assertion of categorical affirmation and added that the Abrahamic Covenant was to be renewed with the second son. Moreover, his name was to be Isaac, meaning "he laughs"; and he was
to be born within a year. To the second question God responded
with blessing for Ishmael, stating that he would indeed be fruitful—that he would be the "father of twelve princes." That promise
was faithfully fulfilled as recorded in Genesis 25:12-16. Ishmael
was not party to the covenant, however: "But my covenant I will
establish with Isaac."

Whatever incredulity and lapse of faith Abraham had evidenced
before, he now demonstrated implicit faith and obedience to God.
Without delay, "on that very day" (v. 23) he saw to it that all the
males of the community were circumcised, thus fulfilling his obligation to the covenant.

NOTES

1. Cyrus Gordon, "Abraham and the Merchants of Ura," *Journal of Near
   Eastern Studies,* January 1958, pp. 28-30.
2. Harold G. Stigers, *A Commentary on Genesis* (Grand Rapids: Zondervan,
   1976), p. 146.

7

ABRAHAM (2)
THE DESTRUCTION OF SODOM

GENESIS 18:1–19:38)

Very soon after Yahweh's appearance to Abraham to confirm the covenant, He appeared to the patriarch again. The proximity of the two events is clear because both 17:21 and 18:10 predict the birth of Isaac within a year. Evidently by that time the quota of iniquity allowed Sodom and the other cities of the plain had been reached (cf. Gen. 15:16), and God had determined to destroy the wicked cities. An important reason God should tell Abraham of His intention was to assure the patriarch that He was not going to blast into infertility the whole land promised to him. Moreover, He wanted to give opportunity for the rescue of Lot and his family.

The contrast in chapters 18 and 19 is tremendous. In the former the holy guests are graciously welcomed, in the latter their very lives are threatened; in the former an obedient, covenant community is blessed, in the latter a vile community is obliterated. An absolutely remarkable feature of the divine visit to Abraham is that God could feel at home with the patriarch and even share with him His thoughts and intents (note especially 18:16-21). Abraham had become a "friend of God" (2 Chron. 20:7; Isa. 41:8; James 2:23; cf. John 15:14-15).

The Visit of the "Three Men" (18:1-15)

Yahweh, God in His covenant relationship, appeared to Abraham at Mamre during the heat of the day, siesta time, when the patriarch was resting and when the travelers should have been resting too. Abraham immediately offered the hospitality so characteristic of Bedouins to the present. There is no evidence that Abraham initially recognized the three to be divine messengers or one of them to be God in human form. As Davis observes, the address of "my lord" (Heb., *Adonai*) was merely a respectful greeting used by others in Scripture (e.g., Jacob, Gen. 32:5; 33:8, 13-15; Joseph's brothers 47:25).[1] The strangers accepted the hospitality, and preparations immediately began for a rather sumptuous meal.

Somehow Abraham must have sensed something very special about those guests because he stood near them while they ate. Custom would have dictated his acting as host and eating with them. Near the end of the meal they inquired about Sarah, evidently by name, which was highly unusual; presumably they had not even been told her name. Sarah was in the women's part of the tent behind a curtain partition; women did not eat with male guests. When Yahweh announced she would have a son by that time next year, she laughed to herself, apparently inaudibly, in incredulity. Either Abraham had not told her about God's previous announcement or he had been unable to convince her that she really would have a son. When accused of laughing by Yahweh, who could read her thoughts (evidence of His deity), she told a boldfaced lie and denied it. But Yahweh rebuffed her, "Yes, you did laugh." The conversation ended and the trio left.

Abraham's Intercession for Sodom (18:16-33)

As the three started their journey in the direction of Sodom, Abraham played the part of a good host and escorted them, apparently for some distance. Along the way, God raised the question of whether He should conceal from Abraham what He was about to do. Probably He thought that to Himself (NEB), though Leupold represents it as a soliloquy spoken loud enough for Abraham to hear.[2] It is unnecessary for the statement to have been audible because God's intent became clearly evident from His statement beginning in verse 20. God's concern seems to have been that the reason for the great destruction about to take place must be conveyed to Abraham so it could serve as a warning to generations to come. The great patriarch could then "enjoin his sons and family after him to keep the way of Yahweh, to practice justice and righteousness." Indeed, he was around to remind of God's requirement for holy living through the 60 years of Isaac until the birth of Jacob and Esau and for the first 15 years of those twin sons. He did not die until 175 years of age (Gen. 25:7).

Yahweh now declares His purpose to investigate the evil of

Sodom and Gomorrah. "The cry of Sodom" seems to refer to the fact that the evil of the place was so heinous as to demand execution of judgment. "I am going down" does not imply that God's omniscience is somehow defective and that it is necessary for Him to collect evidence. Rather, He will inquire in order to demonstrate to men the validity of His judgment. Actually Yahweh went down into the plain but not into Sodom; only the two angels did that. What they saw and experienced as the "eyes of God," abundantly confirmed what God already knew about the depravity of the area.

At this point the two angels moved on toward Sodom and left Abraham alone with God. Abraham "drew near" physically, but more important, his mind and heart reached out to God in intercession. Fully aware that in any massive judgment such as this the righteous would be destroyed with the wicked, Abraham began to plead for sparing the city for the sake of the righteous. Believers can, as salt, be a preservative for society. Though primarily concerned for Lot and his family, Abraham had a larger concern. He began to explore with God how many righteous would have to be found for the city to be spared. He started out with fifty and won the promise that God would spare the whole place for such a number. Something in God's manner might have implied that such a number could not be found. Cautiously Abraham reduced the number to forty-five, taking great care to place himself in proper humility before the Lord, as "dust and ashes," purely transitory in character. Again he won a promise of stay of judgment.

In the course of his prayer the patriarch continued to reduce the number—to forty, thirty, twenty, and ten, each time obtaining a promise to spare the city. He never got so personal or selfish as to pray for relatives only. He stopped at ten, apparently presuming that Lot's influence would guarantee at least that many righteous persons. But evidently such was not the case, as subsequent developments would demonstrate. At the end of the intercession Yahweh "left," no doubt returning to heaven, and Abraham "returned home." Calamity was impending.

Sodom's Wickedness (19:1-14)

The two angels who had visited Abraham continued on to

Sodom and evidently arrived that same evening. The fact that
the journey was some twenty-five miles is of no consequence because those supernatural beings were not limited to the slower
speed of ordinary men. When they arrived at Sodom they met
Lot at the gate. Presumably he had some leadership role in the
city; judges and kings and the city fathers commonly held court
at the gate. If he did become an official there, he may have gained
that position because of relationship to Abraham, who had rescued
the town's inhabitants earlier. Lot prevailed upon the two visitors
to spend the night at his home and generously cared for all their
needs.

Before long a howling mob of men came pounding at the door
demanding the two visitors, so they could have a homosexual
orgy. Their demand in the King James translation is "that we may
know them." That common word refers to sexual relations in numerous places in the Old Testament and evidently does here, because Lot's response is to offer his two daughters to participate in
sexual activity.[3] Jude 7 confirms the sexual connotation. The NIV
translates 19:5 bluntly: "Bring them out to us so that we can
have sex with them." Lot's counteroffer seems unthinkable to a
Western Christian, but it shows the degree to which an ancient
oriental felt obliged to protect his guests. Here a virtue was "in-
flated into a vice"; a parallel offer was made in Judges 19:24.
With the crowd growing more and more ugly and the situation
now obviously out of control, the supernatural visitors stepped in
and afflicted the mob with a form of blindness so they became
completely disoriented and were unable to find the door to break
into Lot's house.

The miracle accredited the divine messengers and their message.
When they announced the impending destruction of Sodom, Lot
believed them. And at their bidding he went out and invited the
young men betrothed to his daughters to flee for their lives. They
"thought he was joking" (NIV) and mocked at the possibility of
God's judgment. The response of the mob and Lot's future sons-
in-law reflect both the weakness of Lot's witness and the callous
nature of the population of Sodom.

Lot's Deliverance (19:15-22)

At dawn the angels urged Lot to take his wife and two daugh-

ters and leave without delay. But the grip of Sodom's materialism
on Lot was too strong. "He hesitated"; so the angels grabbed the
four by the hands and almost dragged them out of the city, "for
Yahweh was sparing them." Having got the quartet out of town,
they issued urgent instructions: "Flee" (speed is of the utmost
importance); "Don't look back" (turn from the evil you are leaving and don't hanker after it); "Don't stop in the plain" (the whole
region is to be wiped out); "Flee to the mountains" (there is a
haven of refuge).

But Lot was too entrapped by the allurements of the town life
of the plain to sever connections completely. Though already
granted great favor from God, he stopped in his moment of extremity to bargain with God. As the fuse on the bomb of judgment burned shorter, he seemed to be pleading that there was not
time to reach the mountain. So he asked permission to settle in
the small town of Bela (Gen. 14:2, 8) which henceforth was
known as Zoar (meaning "small place," v. 22). His emphasis on
the smallness of the place implied that he considered it too small
to have been wicked enough to call down the judgment of God.
In a spirit of remarkable restraint, the angels granted him his
request to go there and to spare the town for his sake. No rebuke
was administered but utmost speed was urged because judgment
was set to fall only after (and immediately after) Lot was safe.
Evidently at that point the angels disappeared.

Destruction of Sodom (19:23-29)

Just as the sun rose and just as Lot reached Zoar, God's hand
of judgment fell. "He rained down burning sulphur and fire" on
the cities of the plain and destroyed the population of the area
and all its vegetation. That is all Scripture says about the catastrophe; it is amazing how concisely biblical writers narrate the
great dramas of history. Penmen with a purely human inspiration would have spiced up those accounts with numerous dramatic
details.

To discuss what may have happened, it is necessary first to locate the cities of judgment. As noted above, Genesis 14:3 states
that the battle of the four kings against the five took place in the
Vale of Siddim, "which is the salt sea." In other words, the vale
subsequently was overflowed by the Dead Sea. Josephus con-

firms the testimony of the biblical reference in saying that with
the disappearance of Sodom the valley has become a lake, "the
so-called Asphaltitis" (his name for the Dead Sea).[4] On these
and other bases, scholars today generally conclude that the cities
of the plain were located at the south end of the Dead Sea and
now lie under its shallow southern extension.

That region is full of combustible material. Some ancient writers spoke of the existence in the plain of asphalt seepages and
boiling waters that emitted foul odors. Great quantities of asphalt
or bitumen appear in the Dead Sea region and continue to rise to
the surface of the water. Seepages of semifluid petroleum still
may be found near the south end of the Dead Sea. J. Penrose
Harland has reconstructed the story of the destruction as follows:
"A great earthquake, perhaps accompanied by lightning, brought
utter ruin and a terrible conflagration to Sodom and the other
communities in the vicinity. The destructive fire may have been
caused by the ignition of gases and seepages of asphalt emanat-
ing from the region, through lightning or the scattering of fires
from hearths."[5] In the explosion of all that combustible material,
burning sulphur and fire would indeed have rained from heaven.
In the massive shaking of the region, the surface of the "vale of
Siddim" may have been further depressed, facilitating the influx
of the waters of the Dead Sea. If God used the natural features of
the region to rain judgment, the primary factor in the miracle was
the time element—"just as Lot reached Zoar."

"Lot's wife looked back" is a simple English translation, but it
cannot convey the sense of the Hebrew. Her sin was not in a
casual, inquisitive glance behind her, but in lingering behind the
others and casting fond glances on what she was leaving behind.
In so doing, she evidently got caught in the eruption and was
covered with molten sulphurous and saline materials and thus
"became a pillar of salt."

Still pondering his remarkable meeting with the heavenly visitor
and greatly concerned about Lot and the city of Sodom, Abraham
got up early the "next morning," the morning after the heavenly
visitation, and thus the same morning that God destroyed the
cities of the plain. He walked to where he had interceded with
Yahweh, evidently a height from which he could at least look in
the direction of Sodom and Gomorrah. Then he saw the sicken-

ing sight, the "dense smoke" ascending from the ruins of the cities of the plain. He had to believe that there were not ten righteous in Sodom. But was Lot rescued? Perhaps he learned some day that he was, but there is no indication from Scripture that they ever saw each other again. At least the sacred historian observes that God "remembered Abraham" and did rescue Lot for his sake.

Lot's Tragedy (19:30-38)

Lot's lack of commitment to and dependence on God had led him to refuse to go to the mountains (19:20); now that lack of faith so filled him with fear that evidently he no longer trusted God to protect Zoar as He had promised (19:21, 30). So he went to the mountains and lived in a cave with his daughters. What a comedown for a man of substance who had chosen the spiritually dangerous, lush plain of the Jordan as a place to live. The frustration of his daughters and their plot to commit incest with their father are clear enough and require no further comment. But the results do. Lot thus became the ancestor of the Moabites and Ammonites, tribes that became inveterate enemies of the Israelites and a great snare to them, in terms of both sexual and religious pollution (e.g., Num. 25:1-5; Lev. 18:21—Molech was an Ammonite deity). Perhaps it would have been better if Lot and his family had perished in the destruction of Sodom.

NOTES

1. John J. Davis, *Paradise to Prison* (Grand Rapids: Baker, 1975), p. 197.
2. H. C. Leupold, *Exposition of Genesis*, 2 vols. (Grand Rapids: Baker, 1942), 1:544.
3. The question of translation here is dealt with adequately in Derek Kidner, *Genesis* (Downers Grove, Ill.: Inter-Varsity, 1967), pp. 136-37. Because the question of whether Scripture really condemns homosexuality is questioned in many circles today, it may be profitable to list a few references for further study: Lev. 18:22, 20:13; Deut. 23:17; 1 Kings 14:24; Rom. 1:21-27; 1 Cor. 6:9; 1 Tim. 1:8-10.
4. Josephus *Antiquities* I. IX.
5. J. Penrose Harland, "Sodom and Gomorrah," Part 2, *Biblical Archaeologist*, September 1943, p. 48.

8

ABRAHAM (3)
COVENANT FULFILLMENT AND LATER
YEARS IN CANAAN

GENESIS 20:1–25:18

Lapse at Gerar (20:1-18)

The spotlight focuses on Abraham once more, and again it exposes his weakness. The patriarch may have been a giant of faith, but he had his moments of faithlessness. Scripture reveals the towering figures of biblical times to have had feet of clay. The effects of man's fallen nature are always present to plague him. It is of course easy to criticize Abraham for his failures, but he really had little to aid him in his daily walk as a believer. There was no written revelation of God that he could consult for instruction for righteous living. And though the Holy Spirit came upon Old Testament saints from time to time to enable them, apparently He did not indwell them on a continuing basis as believers now are indwelt. Thus a great dynamic for spiritual living was missing from Abraham's life.

Critical scholars have thought it inconceivable that Abraham could have again pawned off his wife as a sister and so have treated this passage as a duplicate of Genesis 12. But the circumstances are completely different, and verse 13 reveals that this partial deception was an established arrangement between Abraham and Sarah.

For some reason, perhaps depletion of grazing lands, Abraham moved from the Hebron area into the northern Negev and for a while stayed in Gerar. The location of Gerar is still in doubt, but excavations at Tell Abu Hureira, about eleven miles southeast of Gaza, help to establish it as the site of Gerar. It is some forty miles southwest of Mamre.

Sarah must have been a very remarkable woman indeed to have

appealed to Abimelech as a candidate for his harem at age ninety. That does not mean, however, that she had a child-bearing capability any longer. Such a marriage may have had usefulness for purposes of alliance, as was true of most of Solomon's marriages later on. Abraham had even greater wealth and power now than when he rescued the cities of the plain (Gen. 14).

Of course the real danger in this situation was that if Sarah became Abimelech's wife the Abrahamic Covenant was scuttled; and the line through which the Messiah was to come was eliminated. Therefore God had to step in in dramatic fashion here, as in dealing with Pharaoh, in order to rescue Sarah. He not only appeared to Abimelech in a dream to warn him against violating Sarah, but He also made sterile all the women of Abimelech's household. In order to assure Sarah's return to Abraham, God even threatened Abimelech with death if he kept her. Abraham is described as "a prophet," one who spoke for God or who spoke as an intermediary. In Abimelech's mind that probably signified possession of some magical powers more than holiness of life. Abraham could speak as an official intermediary and completely clear up the present problem before God.

Abimelech pled ignorance and innocence in taking Sarah into his harem, and God accepted his plea. Then perhaps out of fear of Abraham's magical powers, he made him a handsome gift to please him. It served as a "covering of the eyes" to obtain complete "vindication" (v. 16). By making a money gift to Abraham in front of Sarah, he made sure neither of them had any legal claim on him. In accepting the gift, Abraham considered the matter settled; and he prayed to God for the restoration of fertility to Abimelech's family. God did not let Abraham go free without dealing with his lack of trust and his deception, however. The rebuke administered was more stinging when coming from the mouth of a pagan who had a higher sense of morality and fair play than a believer.

Coming of the Promised Heir (21:1-21)

The Birth of Isaac (21:1-7). At last the promised son was born— a long twenty-five years after Abraham had entered the promised land. The heir did not come through adoption (Eliezer) or a concubine (Hagar) but through supernatural involvement with the procreative abilities of Abraham and Sarah. Yahweh's sovereign control over the matter is clearly stated in verses 1 and 2: "as he had said," "what he had promised," "at the time God had promised" (within a year of the visit of the three angels). Abraham's obedience is also indicated in his naming the child Isaac and circumcising him on the eighth day. Isaac (meaning "he laughs") brought the laughter that comes with rejoicing to Sarah and all those dear to her; once the thought of his birth had brought the laughter of incredulity both to her and Abraham.

The birth of the child of the covenant is simply and briefly told, just as was the birth of another promised Son (Christ) in his line almost two millennia later. Yet the effects were to be so profound. His descendants were to be the Hebrew people, who were to change the course of history, through whom was to come the Messiah, Abraham's greater Son, and around whom the events of the end time will swirl.

The Expulsion of Ishmael (21:8-21). When Isaac was two to three years old he was weaned—an important step in his maturing process. On that joyous occasion and apparently in keeping with the custom of the times, Abraham prepared a "great feast." Of course Isaac and his position as Abraham's heir were the center of attention on that occasion. Ishmael, a lad of sixteen or seventeen, looked on—ignored. He who for so long had enjoyed the love and attention of his father now found himself on the outside of things. His pride was hurt; but more than that, he felt suddenly very insecure about his future just as he was growing into adulthood. During the festivities Ishmael was "ridiculing" the helpless infant in whom so much hope now rested.

Sarah, perhaps in anger, but also with insight into what the future held for the household with two such incompatible elements in it, demanded the expulsion of Hagar and Ishmael. Abraham, who loved Ishmael dearly, was grieved at the thought; and it took a command of God for him to acquiesce to Sarah's urging. It is instructive to note that in this conversation both Sarah and God made the point that Isaac, not Ishmael, was the true heir. In the Semitic society from which Abraham came, if a man fathered children by a slave girl, they were not to share in his estate along with his wife and legitimate sons, if such were born to the first-rank wife. Moreover, children born of a slave and their mother were to be given their freedom; they could not be kept in slavery after the man died. That is spelled out in the Code of Hammurabi, Law 171. If it is assumed that that proviso operated in Hebrew relationships, Hagar and Ishmael could not have been held in the household indefinitely anyway; and it does not appear to be so cruel that Abraham should expel them at that time. Moreover, there is nothing Abraham or Hagar and Ishmael had to fear when God's protecting and providing care was promised. In Galatians 4:21-31 Hagar and her son are made to stand for the bondage of Mount Sinai and Sarah and her son to stand for freedom in grace; the former is to be expelled.

Assured by God of the rightness of his action, Abraham sent Hagar and Ishmael away with a skin (probably a goat skin) full of water and some food. Nothing else is mentioned. Presumably they also carried extra clothing and possibly some gold or silver. As a lad of about seventeen, Ishmael could have carried a fair amount. Only the food and water are mentioned because the emphasis in this passage is on sustenance. Instead of attaching themselves to a band traveling somewhere, the pair "strayed about in the desert of Beersheba," the relatively uninhabited northern Negev where water was sparse. Presumably they got lost, ran out of provisions, and decided the end had come. Hagar pushed or dragged Ishmael under a bush to protect him from the broiling sun and went some distance away to avoid seeing him die and hearing his dying moans.

While Hagar sobbed, Ishmael apparently cried for help— whether to God or man, it is not clear. In any case, God heard the boy, and His angel called to Hagar who seems to have been in better shape at the moment. Perhaps his question should be translated, "What ails you?" as if referring to the promise made to Hagar earlier that some day she would have many descendants (Gen. 16:10). He might have said, "Don't you have any faith in My promises?" Then He reiterated the promise to her and "opened her eyes" to see a "well of water," either providing water miraculously or pointing her to a supply she had not noticed before. The narrative now skips rapidly over the rest of Ishmael's life, noting only that he enjoyed God's watchcare, that he became expert in the use of the bow, and that he lived in the Wilderness of Paran. This region seems to have extended through the northwest part

of the Sinai peninsula and the area south of the Dead Sea. His
mother secured a wife for him from Egypt, and he had twelve sons
(Gen. 25:16).

Covenant with Abimelech (21:22-34)

At some point after Abraham's earlier involvement with Abimelech at Gerar (chap. 20), the patriarch moved about twenty-five
miles southeast to the vicinity of Beersheba. There the more recent events had occurred; from there Hagar and Ishmael had
been expelled to wander in the nearby desert. "At that time"
(evidently of Hagar's expulsion) Abimelech and his army com-
mander, Phicol, came to make some sort of an agreement with
Abraham. Apparently Abimelech's sphere of influence extended
to the vicinity of Beersheba; and he wanted to insure peaceful
coexistence with Abraham, whose wealth and power were increasing rapidly ("God is with you in whatever you do"). Abimelech's
request that Abraham swear to a covenant or treaty before Elohim
implies that Abimelech had considerable respect for Abraham's
God—at least enough to consider a covenant made before Him to
be binding. Then in the negotiations Abimelech reminded Abraham that he had a right to expect that Abraham would recipro-
cate the kindness he had shown the patriarch.

Abraham acceded to the request, but before concluding the
covenant "complained" about the seizure of a well by Abimelech's
servants. That was no small matter in an area where water was
precious, but Abimelech evidently wanted nothing to stand in the
way of the covenant and sought to dismiss the matter quickly.
The treaty proper was concluded and what amounted to a codicil
was added specifying that the seized well belonged to Abraham.
So the place was called "Beersheba," which may mean "well of
seven" (the seven lambs given in token of ownership) or "well
of swearing." Then Abimelech and Phicol returned to the "land of
the Philistines" and Abraham continued to live on the edge of
that land.

Many argue that mention of the Philistines here is anachronistic,
though they are mentioned again in Genesis 26:1, 8, 14, 15, 18.
They hold that the Philistines arrived in Palestine early in the
twelfth century, only after being repulsed by the Egyptians.
Though warlike bands of Philistines did indeed hit the Palestinian

coast in the twelfth century and subjugated much of the land, there is no reason groups of more peaceful Philistines may not have arrived much earlier. If Caphtor, the home of the Philistines (Jer. 47:4; Amos 9:7), is to be identified with Crete (as is commonly held), two waves of Philistines may have come to Palestine: peaceful commercial Minoans early in the second millennium (during the patriarchal period) and more warlike Mycenaeans in the latter part of the millennium (during the days of the Judges).

Offering of Isaac (22:1-24)

"Some time later," perhaps when Isaac was ten or twelve, God "tested" or sought to prove Abraham's faith. He demanded the supreme sacrifice, the life of Isaac. And God made it clear that He understood the magnitude of the demand He was making: "Your only son . . . whom you love." Of course it was a wrenching command, one that would cause Abraham's heart almost literally to bleed. But whatever anguish he suffered, he did not enter into any prolonged debate with God. Promptly, "early the next morning," he obeyed completely. Through the many steps of his development he had learned to trust God implicitly and to count on His miracle-working power. Hebrews 11:17-19 reveals that Abraham obeyed God so unequivocally in this instance because he expected that, if necessary, God would raise Isaac from the dead. After all, God had explicitly promised that the covenant was to be fulfilled in Isaac (Gen. 21:12); he was to be the father of a vast multitude, and he could not be if allowed to remain in the grave.

In obedience, Abraham made his way to Moriah, the northeastern hill of Jerusalem on which Solomon later was to build the Temple (2 Chron. 3:1). It took the party three days to travel the approximately fifty miles from Beersheba to Jerusalem. When reached, the sacrifice spot was almost within eyesight of Calvary, where another supreme sacrifice could not be arrested as this one was to be. It is significant that as Abraham approached Mount Moriah and commanded his servants to wait for him and Isaac at a designated spot, he said "We *will* come back to you." The Hebrews reference already noted is evidence that that assertion was not merely small talk or an effort on Abraham's part to avoid telling them what was about to take place. Moreover, his expectation that God would do something miraculous was demonstrated by his plan to return home promptly; presumably he would not have dared to face Sarah again if he were to destroy Isaac.

At length Isaac began to wonder where the sacrificial animal was; in faith Abraham assured him that God would provide. But soon it became clear to Isaac the part he was to play in this drama. Certainly he was big enough to have run away from his aged father, but there is no hint of resistance. No doubt his father had rehearsed with him many times the fact that he was to participate fully in the blessings of the Abrahamic Covenant and to be the father of many. Faith in that promise helped to carry Isaac through this test too. The whole scene is magnificently illustrative of the tremendous sacrifice of the heavenly Father in offering His Son and the obedience of the Son in submitting to a sacrificial death. Suddenly God intervened and stopped the whole proceeding; He provided a ram as a substitute, but there was to be no substitute for the greater Son whose sacrifice this event portrayed. Abraham's faith had been proved, had matured. And the spiritual children of this father of the faithful need to be reminded that their commitment, like his, is to be total. Such faith in Yahweh-Yireh, "the Lord who provides," gives strength to face the crises of life, both big and small.

In approval of Abraham's total devotion, God reiterated the covenant made earlier but added the element that Abraham's descendants would "take possession of the gates of their enemies." That may refer to the conquest under Joshua but probably has a broader implication of victory in subsequent periods and perhaps looks forward to a glorious future day when Abraham's greater Son will have made His enemies and all evil His footstool. From the inspired elaboration in Galatians 3:16, it is clear that the "seed" referred to in Genesis 22:18 specifically anticipates the coming of Christ.

The genealogical reference at the end of the chapter at first glance seems unrelated to what has been going on, but such is not the case. Not only would God bring to pass His purposes through Abraham and Isaac; but hundreds of miles away He also had been in the process of raising up Rebekah the one who would share Isaac's life and through whom the covenant fulfillment would be advanced.

Death and Burial of Sarah (23:1-20)

Sarah died at the age of 127; Abraham was 137 at the time and Isaac 37. The family had moved back to the Hebron area from Beersheba; so an effort to find a burial place for Sarah did not involve Philistines but Hittites instead.

To the assertion that Hittites could not have entered Canaan that early because it was centuries before the establishment of the Hittite kingdom and empire in Asia Minor, it may be answered that there were various stages of Hittite development. Long before Indo-Europeans crossed over from Europe to Asia Minor (about 2000 B.C.) to begin the process that was to culminate in the Hittite kingdom, non-Indo-European sons of Heth (Hittites) lived in the region. Apparently some of those settled as far south as Hebron. There is no valid reason for assuming, as many do, that Scripture is historically inaccurate in its reference to the Hittites here.

The primary question at this point was whether or not Abraham, an "alien and stranger" in the land, was to be given an opportunity to gain property rights. The negotiations began with a Hittite offer to let him use a tomb on someone's land. Abraham countered with a desire to buy property (a first step in gaining title to it) and identified a marketable parcel owned by Ephron. He asked for help from the men of the community in persuading Ephron to sell it. Then Abraham offered to buy a cave for burial purposes on the edge of Ephron's land. Ephron countered with the idea that the field was to go with the cave. His offer to give the property to Abraham was only an oriental way of bargaining; he had no intention of giving away anything so valuable. When Abraham insisted on buying a burial plot and promised to pay the full market price, Ephron named what seems to be a rather steep price. Apparently he took advantage of Abraham's need and his ability to pay. Abraham had no real choice but to pay what was demanded. The price named came at the end of the bargaining process rather than at the beginning of it; hence there was no haggling over the matter.

Since this was more than a millennium before the coinage of money, payment was by means of bullion weighed out. That Abraham had that kind of liquid wealth on hand shows he was not merely a Bedouin sheep-or goatherd. Cyrus Gordon concluded that he was a merchant prince.[1] The deal was finalized in the typical manner of ancient times in Palestine: elders of the town witnessed the transaction at the gate of the city, and the property was officially deeded over to Abraham.

So Abraham buried Sarah in the cave of Machpelah at Hebron. Subsequently Abraham was buried there (Gen. 25:9); and later, Isaac, Rebekah, and Leah (Gen. 49:31); and later yet, Jacob (Gen. 50:13). Today the mosque of Hebron stands over the traditional site of the cave, and cenotaphs inside the mosque commemorate the burials that presumably were made below. Since both Arabs and Jews claim Abraham as father, the spot is one of the most highly revered in the world.

A Bride for Isaac (24:1-67)

When Abraham was "old," actually 140 (see Gen. 21:5 and 25:20), he became concerned that he had not yet arranged for the marriage of Isaac (then forty). If his posterity were to be guaranteed and the covenant fulfilled, a bride must be found for Isaac. If Abraham did not find a suitable God-fearing woman before he died, others might contract for a marriage to a Canaanite after his demise. Therefore he charged his "chief" or "oldest" servant (possibly Eliezer, though he would have been very aged by that time) to go to northern Mesopotamia to locate a bride among relatives in the region of Haran. Abraham sought to put his steward under oath that he would faithfully perform this task. Verse 2 shows how such solemn oaths were made between men; "under the thigh" may be under the genitals, the seat of procreative powers. That act would be significantly symbolic in this instance, for success of the mission would make possible propagation of posterity and fulfillment of the Abrahamic Covenant.

Abraham agreed that refusal of a bride to return with the servant would release him from his oath. But he could not entertain thoughts of failure of the venture because the God who had promised him the land of Canaan would surely grant success. Twice (vv. 6, 8) he warned against taking Isaac back to Mesopotamia, for fear that Isaac would fail to return to the promised land.

Without delay the servant prepared for the journey and set out for northern Mesopotamia. The selection of ten camels from the herd implies a much larger number and helps to underscore Abraham's great wealth. Though in the past scholars have questioned that Abraham had camels at all or that they were domesticated that early, there seems now to be no reasonable doubt about their availability.[2]

It is instructive to see how Abraham's servant proceeded when he reached his destination. First, he bathed the project in prayer. His prayer was to the "God of my master Abraham." Evidently he had become a follower of God because of the witness of Abraham; sometimes others do put their trust in God because of our faithfulness to Him. But the servant did not worship God only because He was the deity honored in the household of Abraham; he himself evidently was on intimate terms with God. Second, he proposed a test. Though God cannot be expected to act every time a believer puts out a "fleece" or proposes special means for determining His will, sometimes He does respond positively to the tests put forward by the desperately sincere. And without getting involved in the whole argument of free will versus predetermination, it may be suggested that at least sometimes God puts such thoughts in our minds as a means of getting His purposes accomplished. At any rate, God answered that particular prayer.

Abraham's servant had, in effect, prayed that God would identify the bride of His choice by having the maiden addressed offer water both to himself and his camels. And there he was at the well, where women of the ancient Near East came in the cool of the day to draw water for the family needs during the day ahead, and perhaps to exchange a bit of gossip. How shall he decide whom to approach? There was a young woman with striking physical attributes. Was her beauty only skin deep? Was she proud and lazy and in other ways unacceptable as a bride for Isaac? There was a way to find out—ask her the leading question. The test was not capricious but wise. In the process of watching Rebekah's response the servant learned a lot about her. She was outgoing, able to meet strangers graciously and to put them at ease. She was also courteous and industrious—important qualities for one who was to manage Isaac's household. As Rebekah busied herself with ministering to the needs of the strangers, the servant looked on in tense silence and "scrutinized her" to decide whether or not she was really the sought-for bride. When she finished, he gave her a gift (putting the ornaments on her, v. 47), perhaps only

[handwritten annotation: Torah / ABRAM NAHOR — REBECCA / BETHUEL — LABAN]

in gratitude for her actions. She had passed the test, but was she of Abraham's people and would there be a reception for the servant in her home? She turned out to be a granddaughter of Nahor, Abraham's brother (cf. Gen. 11:27); and she assured the strangers that there was "plenty" of provender for the animals and room for the guests.

The servant was overwhelmed with gratitude at the rapid turn of events. His first thought was of God ("praise"), his second of his master, and his third of himself and the success of his venture. God had indeed sent His angel on ahead, as Abraham had confidently predicted (v. 7); and He had prepared the hearts of all concerned, as was about to become evident.

Rebekah left the servant by the well while she quickly ran to bring news of his arrival and to arrange for his proper care. The fact that she reported to her "mother's household" indicates that her father was a polygamist; the eldest of each set of children had special responsibility for the rest. In that case, Laban, Rebekah's brother, did the honors. Of course he would fulfill the requirements of oriental courtesy, but he was especially prompted by the richness of the gift to Rebekah (v. 30). That reference seems to imply something of the cupidity of Laban and to anticipate his later efforts to take advantage of Jacob in every way he could. Laban then hurried out to extend a more formal invitation to Abraham's servant to come with his party and animals to spend the night.

Next the customary oriental amenities were provided: care for the animals, water for the servant and his men to wash their feet (to cleanse away the dirt from the dusty road and to soothe their tired and aching condition), and a meal. At that point the customary procedure was interrupted; normally the meal would have been concluded and then business discussed. The servant insisted on conducting business first and was granted his wish.

After introducing himself, he opened the appeal for Rebekah's hand in marriage in a very impressive way: Abraham had become very wealthy; he had an only son to whom he had given his entire estate, and he had ordered that a bride be found for his son from his God-fearing relatives rather than the pagan Canaanites. The servant continued in a quite different vein, indicating that Abraham had assured him of God's prospering his venture, and recounting that God had indeed clearly shown in the scene at the well that Rebekah was His choice for Isaac. The match had been made in heaven. Having stated his case, the servant in effect called on Rebekah's family to share in the purposes of God. He had demonstrated the material wealth of the groom and the direction of God in the matter; he applied no further pressure.

Laban and his father Bethuel bowed in obedience to what seemed to be the clearly-revealed will of God—a response to be expected from the people of God. The betrothal was completed; and according to custom, the servant then presented to the bride the rich gifts sent by the bridegroom. What he next gave to the bride's family may be interpreted as the bride-price. In gratitude to God for a mission successfully completed, the servant prayed to God for the third time (vv. 12, 26, 52). Truly he was a man of faith and trust. With mission accomplished, it was now time to eat and sleep.

Again the next morning the servant's urgency was pressed. He wanted to take Rebekah and leave for home immediately, but her brother and mother countered with a delaying tactic. When the servant was insistent, the decision was left up to Rebekah. She agreed to go. The account is reported tersely and without emotional embellishment, but the tugs on the heart must have been great indeed. A young girl who had lived a sheltered life was suddenly confronted with a marriage proposal and the immediate departure for a faraway land, probably never to see any of her family again. In her heart Rebekah must have been saying to Isaac something similar to what Ruth said to Naomi: "Where you go, I will go, and where you lodge, I will lodge. Your people shall be my people, and your God, my God" (Ruth 1:16, NASB*).

In that difficult moment Rebekah's faith sustained her, but human support was available too. Her nurse and some maidens went along. The nurse, Deborah, was destined to be a faithful companion indeed and finally died in the household of Jacob at Bethel (Gen. 35:8). The family also sent her on her way with a blessing, which must not be regarded as a mere pious wish but a belief in God's fulfillment of His covenant promises. Evidently they had some understanding of what God was doing through Abraham, and it was their degree of faith in God that had commended them

*New American Standard Bible.

to Abraham as a source of a bride for Isaac. They hoped Rebekah would have numerous descendants who ultimately would "possess the gates of their enemies," that is, triumph over them—a prophecy that seems to look forward to the millennial period for complete fulfillment.

The narrative skips over the details of the journey south and picks up again as the caravan neared its destination. Isaac had moved from Beersheba to *Beer-lahai-roi* (meaning "well of the Living One who sees me"), a site unknown but possibly about fifty miles southwest of Beersheba (Gen. 25:11). Seemingly he had set up his own camp at least partially separate from that of Abraham. The caravan came upon him while he was out in a field where he had gone to "meditate" or "pray." The meaning of the Hebrew is uncertain but "meditate" seems to be the intent. The subject of Isaac's thoughts is not stated, but certainly he must have been exercised about the success of the servant's venture and the kind of bride obtained for him.

Just at that moment the servant and the bride appeared on the horizon. Because, according to custom, a woman should wear a veil when in the presence of men not of the household or before a man she was about to marry, Rebekah veiled herself. The servant gave a full report of his doings, which certainly included an adequate recounting of God's superintendence of the whole endeavor. Isaac needed such assurance, as did Rebekah, especially because the couple was destined to wait for twenty years before a child would come along to fulfill the covenant promise. Rebekah "comforted" Isaac; in other words, she filled up the void left by his mother's death.

The Death of Abraham (25:1-18)

The death of Abraham is described in connection with a listing of the families that sprang from him. From this passage it becomes abundantly clear that he did indeed become the father of many nations (Gen. 17:4). But it is equally clear that none of those descendants was to be considered a son of the covenant except Isaac. Those men are spoken of as sons of Keturah or of Hagar. Abraham left his entire estate to Isaac (v. 5); but he gave gifts to the other sons and sent them away during his lifetime so they would not be around to make claims as heirs after he died. Whether reference to "concubines" (v. 6) applies to Keturah and

Hagar only or includes other unnamed women may be left open to question, but presumably the former is true. The translation of 25:1 apparently should read, "Abraham had taken another wife," that is, before the death of Sarah. This conclusion is reached from the fact that Keturah is called a concubine in verse 6 and 1 Chronicles 1:32. If Sarah were dead, Keturah consistently should have been called a wife. Moreover, presumably Abraham's physical powers were too diminished by the time of Sarah's death for him to have fathered additional children (24:1). He was close to 140 when Sarah died. The six sons of Keturah and their descendants occupied territory in the Sinai, Arabia, Transjordan, and south of the Dead Sea. It is beyond the scope of this study to discuss those tribal relations and their locations. Suffice it to say that the Asshurim or Asshurites are not to be confused with the Assyrians; possibly they are to be located south of Mecca in the Arabian peninsula.

Ishmael, like Jacob, had twelve sons who became "tribal chiefs." They and their descendants settled in the Arabian peninsula and somewhat overlapped the territory occupied by descendants of Keturah and must have intermarried with them. The last half of verse 18 is problematical but probably is to be translated in the spirit, if not in the exact words of the NIV: "and they lived in hostility toward all their brothers." Reference, then, would be to the condition of endemic conflict that has existed between the clans and tribes of Arabia even into modern times. Ishmael was 137 when he died.

But he was over 85 and Isaac 76 when the pair buried their father Abraham alongside Sarah in the cave of Machpelah at Hebron. Abraham was 175 at his death and thus lived to a ripe old age as God had predicted (15:15). Moreover, he lived to have not only a son in fulfillment of the covenant but also a grandson. Jacob, who would beget the progenitors of the twelve tribes of Israel, was fifteen when Abraham died. The two half-brothers, Isaac and Ishmael, were able to put aside their animosity toward each other long enough to participate in the funeral of their father.

NOTES

1. Cyrus Gordon, "Abraham and the Merchants of Ura," *Journal of Near Eastern Studies,* January 1958, pp. 28-30.
2. Joseph P. Free, "Abraham's Camels," *Journal of Near Eastern Studies,* July 1944, pp. 187-93.

9

ISAAC

GENESIS 25:19–26:35

Isaac is somewhat obscured by the more eventful lives of his father and his son. He grew up in the shadow of a godly father and in the memory of his offering on Mount Moriah. He seems to have been a very devout man, and God confirmed to him the covenant made to Abraham. Like his father he was forced to wait a very long time for the birth of an heir. And like his father he became entangled with Abimelech in Gerar and passed off his wife as his sister.

But Isaac was also very much unlike his father. He never traveled more than a few miles from his birthplace. He had only one wife and she bore him only two children. He had no spirit of aggression or self-assertion and was never in a battle. He became blind in his old age and nearly helpless and lived to be 180 years old, whereas Abraham died at the age of 175.

Though there were very few stirring events in Isaac's biography, he had his share of trials. As a young child he suffered the persecution of his older brother Ishmael. As a lad he endured the sacrifice on Mount Moriah. He was very close to his mother and evidently grieved for her some years after her death. An especially great trial was the extended barrenness of Rebekah. Then at 75 he suffered the death of his father and subsequently endured a severe famine, which sent him into the land of the Philistines. Esau's marriage to two idolatrous women caused Isaac and Rebekah great grief; Esau was, after all, the eldest son and Isaac's favorite and presumably the child of promise. Next Isaac began to go blind, and when blind he suffered the great deception perpetrated on him by his wife and Jacob. As a result he gave the oral blessing to Jacob. Later he suffered the exile of Jacob, the death of Rebekah, and the departure of Esau. Isaac took his sorrows gracefully. He was an intensely religious, domestic, and peaceful man.

The Birth of an Heir (25:19-26)

As was true with his father Abraham, Isaac was destined to wait a very long time for the birth of an heir. Abraham waited for and anguished over the provision of the child of covenant promise more than twenty-five years. Isaac was forced to wait twenty years; he was forty when he married (25:20) and sixty when Jacob and Esau were born (25:26). Isaac "prayed for" or "entreated" God on behalf of his barren wife. Had God not promised Abraham that from Isaac his descendants would come (21:10)? Perhaps Isaac now reminded God of that commitment. In the extended barrenness of both Sarah and Rebekah and divine intervention to provide an heir, evidently God wanted to make it clear that the covenant child was both divine and omnipotently given; he was not merely a product of natural processes.

Then when conception finally occurred, Rebekah bore twins that "struggled" or "jostled" or "clashed" in her womb. Greatly perplexed about her condition, Rebekah went to Yahweh to inquire of the meaning of what she was experiencing. The explanation was clear and specific. Two babies within her womb would become the ancestors of two peoples (Esau of the Edomites and Jacob of the Israelites). Evidently both the children and their descendants would contest for the mastery. But the contest would be especially great between the children themselves, and the younger would come out on top. But that reversal of the natural order of giving primacy to the firstborn would not occur because of the greater strength or abilities of the younger. Nor was the prediction merely a product of God's foreknowledge. Romans 9:10-12 makes it clear that God's sovereign choice was involved, a choice that had nothing to do with the relative merits of the twins, because the decision had been made before their birth.

Presumably Rebekah reported that divine explanation and pronouncement to Isaac, and possibly Esau and Jacob knew about it later. Knowing that they had a serious problem of child-rearing on their hands, Isaac and Rebekah should have exercised greater wisdom than they did. Unfortunately, partiality always characterized the household: Isaac favored Esau and treated him as the heir, and Rebekah favored Jacob.

In due time the twins were born. The first appeared "red" and "hairy all over like a hair-cloak" (NEB); so he was called Esau, which means "hairy." The second male infant appeared immediately, grasping his brother's heel. So they called him Jacob, which means "heel-gripper" or "one that takes by the heel" or "supplanter." His action at birth characterized his tenacity in striving to secure the birthright or his activities as a supplanter. When the boys were born, grandfather Abraham was 160, as noted above. No doubt it strengthened his faith to see a grandchild born in the line of promise, but two descendants—Isaac and Jacob—were a far cry from the realization of God's assurance that his progeny would be as numerous as the "dust of the earth" (Gen. 13:16).

Esau's Sale of His Birthright (25:27-34)

As Jacob and Esau grew up, they were clearly different in every way—not only in physical characteristics but also in temperament and activities. Esau was a rough outdoorsman and an excellent hunter, whereas Jacob was a "plain" or "quiet" or "cultured" man who "led a settled life and stayed among the tents" (NEB). Isaac came to favor Esau, both because he was the firstborn and should be the heir and because he very much appreciated the game he caught. Rebekah favored Jacob, presumably because he was God's choice as covenant heir and because she found it easier to identify with his life-style.

Once when Esau returned from hunting, he was utterly famished as he came upon Jacob cooking a lentil stew, probably mixed with onions and garlic. Esau was seized with an almost uncontrollable passion to have some of the red stuff. His love for the red lentil stew is given as a reason he was also called Edom ("red," v. 30). Of course he could have been called Edom because of the ruddy appearance with which he had been born.

Taking advantage of the situation, Jacob demanded that Esau sell his birthright for the lentil stew. In patriarchal society, possession of the birthright involved headship of the family, priestly function in the family, and, at a later time at least, a double portion of the inheritance (Deut. 21:17). In addition, in this case it included possession of the covenant promises. Presumably Jacob knew from his mother that he was destined to be the child of the covenant, rather than Esau. Jacob's sin in the transaction was threefold: (1) presumptive toward God in trying to hurry up the fulfillment of His purposes; (2) unfilial toward Isaac in trying to take the birthright from his elder, favored son; (3) unfraternal toward Esau in trying to take advantage of his extremity.

Esau's sin lay in that (1) he was sensual and materialistic; he sacrificed the future on the altar of the immediate; (2) he despised the birthright and was, according to Hebrews 12:16, "profane" (KJV) or "godless" (NIV) or "worldly-minded" (NEB). Though the Genesis narrative does not excuse Jacob for his actions, the real condemnation fell on Esau. Presumably the boys had discussed the birthright on prior occasions, and Esau had shown a sufficiently careless attitude so as to encourage Jacob to believe he could get away with such a one-sided bargain. And he did! That it was possible to sell a birthright in the patriarchal society is clear from texts found at Nuzi in northern Mesopotamia.

Isaac and Abimelech (26:1-16)

Textual critics frequently assume that there was one account of a patriarch's passing off his wife as his sister and that the editors of the source documents became confused and assigned the action to Abraham twice (chap. 12 and 20) and to his son Isaac (chap. 26). But as noted earlier, Abraham arranged with his wife to pass as his sister under certain circumstances, and evidently she did on at least two occasions. Further, there is no reason to conclude that a son would be immune from following a course of action similar to that of his father. Moreover, 26:1 specifically distinguishes this event in Isaac's life from one of those in Abraham's life: "besides the earlier famine which arose in Abraham's time" (cf. Gen. 12:10). Also, there were important differences between Abraham's lapse and that of Isaac. For example, Rebekah was not taken from her husband as Sarah was, and there was no miracle of warning or judgment in this chapter as there was in Abraham's case.

Confronted with a famine in the semi-arid region near Kadesh-Barnea, Isaac panicked and trekked about fifty miles northeastward to Gerar in Philistine territory, which enjoyed greater rainfall. There another Abimelech was ruling, likely a son or grandson of the one who was king in Abraham's day (cf. Gen. 20:2); evidently that was a recurring family name. Temporarily Isaac seems to have lost his faith in God to provide for him and he acted on his own to meet his needs. Moreover, he even made plans to leave the

promised land for Egypt in an effort to enjoy greater material
security. God moved to forestall such a venture and appeared to
Isaac with another confirmation of the Abrahamic Covenant. Isaac
would not have gone north in order to move south into Egypt; so
perhaps he determined to travel to Egypt after an initial cool reception at Gerar.

God commanded Isaac to "stay in the land" and then promised
immediate and long-range blessings to Isaac and his descendants.
He would meet Isaac's needs, would grant him an innumerable
posterity and would give them possession of "all these lands" (vv.
3-4), the *promised land,* inhabited by the various peoples enu-
merated in Genesis 15:19-21. Moreover, through his "offspring,"
notably the Messiah, the blessing of God would come to "all peoples of the earth." This was the repetition of the Abrahamic
Covenant to Abraham's heir and probably was the first time God
spoke to him so directly. Although the covenant made to Abraham
was purely of grace and was unconditional, Abraham's total and
unequivocal obedience (indicated in the heaping up of similar
terms in v. 5) in some sense ratified or clinched the covenant's
operation. God's promises may be sure, but they do not give men
license to do as they please. Isaac obeyed and stayed in Canaan,
but possibly God's command did not mean he should have remained among the Philistines. Such a course of action was fraught
with difficulty; perhaps he should have gone back to Beersheba or
somewhere else to the south.

Isaac's faith in God to supply his needs was quickly tainted with
the sin of lying because of fear for his personal safety. Concerned
that the Philistines might seek to kill him in order to get hold of
his beautiful wife, Isaac passed her off as his sister, as his father
had done with Sarah, and thus put Rebekah in jeopardy. Stigers
points out that according to the customs of northern Mesopotamia,
from which Rebekah had come, a man's wife was his legal sister;
therefore Isaac technically was not guilty of telling a lie. But
Philistine ignorance of that fact made him guilty of gross deception.[1]

After "a long time," during which no one molested either Rebekah or Isaac, Abimelech happened to look out a window one
day to see Isaac "fondling" his wife. Discovering the truth of their
relationship, Abimelech summoned Isaac to make him account for

his deception. The consternation and the orders of Abimelech in verses 10-11 reflect a high moral code among that group of Philistines or possibly a fear implanted during Abraham's lapse at Gerar (Gen. 20:7). Abimelech then graciously permitted Isaac to remain in his territory, where God greatly prospered him. On the surface it would appear that God blessed the sin of Isaac, but such is not the case. Promising to care for him in the promised land, God had instructed him not to go down into Egypt but to remain in Canaan. Isaac had obeyed and God kept His commitment. In the process the sin of the patriarch was exposed and publicly condemned; God never varnishes over the faults of His chosen ones.

In time God used the prosperity of Isaac to move him out of the locale in which he probably should never have been in the first place. The Philistines became envious of Isaac's prosperity, and resources of the region seem not to have been sufficient for both his livestock and that of the Philistines. The Philistines stopped up wells on which Isaac depended, and Abimelech asked him to leave. The assertion that the Hebrews had become "too strong for us" indicates that the Philistines of that early period may not have been very numerous or powerful.

Strife over Wells (26:17-33)

When Isaac left Gerar, evidently he did so reluctantly and remained in the general vicinity—in the Valley of Gerar. Because his large herds required a lot of water, he cleared the wells that Abraham had dug and that the Philistines had stopped up. In the process his servants discovered a natural flowing well of fresh water—a great prize in that region. Because the well was dug in land under their jurisdiction, the Philistines claimed rights to it. As a result of the contention, Isaac named the well *Esek* (meaning "strife"). When Isaac dug a second well a little distance away, the Philistines sought to control that also; Isaac named it *Sitnah* ("opposition"). Moving farther yet from Gerar, Isaac dug a third well, which was uncontested because evidently it lay beyond Philistine territorial limits. Therefore Isaac named it *Rehoboth* (meaning "broad spaces" or "living room"); they now had room to expand. Rehoboth has been identified with Ruheibeh, about nineteen miles southwest of Beersheba. For some reason Rehoboth proved unsatisfactory and Isaac returned to Beersheba; presumably the famine was over.

The very night Isaac returned to Beersheba, God appeared to him to give assurance. "Stop fearing." Isaac had feared inadequate food supply, personal danger, Philistine herdsmen, and the continuing failure to see any descendants. God promised His presence, provision, and posterity. The spot where God appeared became especially sacred; so Isaac built an altar, offered a sacrifice, and settled down there. Naturally if he were to remain there, adequate water supply was required; so his servants began to dig for water.

Soon Abimelech and two of his leading men came to Isaac in Beersheba to make a covenant with him, much the same as the Philistines had in Abraham's day (Gen. 21:22-34). The covenant was of value first to Abimelech because it assured him of the good will of Isaac, who evidently was a rising power, and because it eliminated the danger of affront to Isaac's God. Second, it was of value to Isaac because it removed any threat the Philistines posed and because it assured him of the blessing of God. In fact, what comes through loud and clear in the Philistine speech is their impression that "Yahweh is with thee."

At the beginning of the negotiations Isaac administered a gentle rebuke, asking why they were coming to him, "seeing that you on your part were hostile to me and drove me away." The intimation is that enmity was and is entirely on their side: "you on your part." Their response is conciliatory: "We did not touch you"; "we have done only good to you"; "we sent you away in peace." As a matter of fact, those leaders may have had no part in the squabble of herdsmen and therefore could claim innocence in the animosities of the past. In any case, conditions were different now. The Philistines proposed a covenant of peace between them, and Isaac accepted and sealed the agreement with a covenant-feast as a token of good will. That very day Isaac's servants came with the report that they had found water in the well they had been digging. So the patriarch had a peace covenant and assurance of an adequate water supply all in one day. He decided to call the well *Shibah* ("oath") and to call the settlement *Beersheba* ("well of the oath or covenant"), even as Abraham had called it *Beersheba* ("well of oath or well of the seven," Gen. 21:

30-31), referring to the "sevening" of themselves by means of the seven lambs.

Esau's Marriages (26:34-35)

At first glance these verses may seem slightly out of place, but that is not the case. Earlier the inadequacies of Esau's nature have been introduced; now his failure in marriage is noted. Both disqualify him to be the heir to the Abrahamic Covenant. That disqualification needs to be clear before the spotlight focuses on Jacob as the heir during the next several chapters. And that marriage note serves as a prelude to Jacob's search for a wife among his own people (27:46—28:4). Esau's marriage took place at age forty to pagan Hittite wives, instead of following the pattern set by Abraham in chapter 24: marriage to God-fearing kinfold. The "bitterness of spirit" that came to Isaac and Rebekah from those marriages would rise from the heathen corruption brought into the family by that means. And for Isaac, who still sought to make Esau his heir, there was great consternation over how the covenant and its provisions would fare in such a family and among its descendants.

NOTES

1. Harold G. Stigers, *A Commentary on Genesis* (Grand Rapids: Zondervan, 1976), p. 213.

10

JACOB (1)
EARLY YEARS AND SOJOURN IN HARAN

GENESIS 27:1–30:43

Jacob (meaning "supplanter") truly lived up to his name, first persuading his brother Esau to sell his birthright and then deceiving his father and stealing the oral blessing. But when Jacob went to the home of his mother's brother Laban in search of a wife, he more than met his match in craftiness. Ultimately, he worked for Laban fourteen years for his wives Leah and Rachel, and six years for the flocks and herds obtained from Laban.

Often the question is asked why God would bless such a scoundrel as Jacob, seeming even to reward his evil ways. By way of answer, it should be remembered that God calls followers not because of what they are but for what they may become by His grace. No one deserves the blessings of God. Second, God had made an unconditional covenant with Abraham and confirmed it to Isaac; that involved working through the natural descendants of Isaac, that is Jacob. Third, however dimly, Jacob apparently had some appreciation of the spiritual blessings of God's covenant. And on the way to Laban's home in northern Mesopotamia, he stopped at Bethel, sacred as a shrine of his grandfather Abraham. There God revealed Himself to Jacob and confirmed the Abrahamic Covenant to him, without any indication that He approved of all his actions (Gen. 28:10-22). Fourth, Jacob was exiled from home for his deception of Isaac and endured many maturing situations during the twenty years in exile. Fifth, a chastened man, he met God in a spiritually revolutionizing way along the banks of the Jabbok River on the journey home (Gen. 32). Then God changed his name to *Israel* ("fighter for God"). Sixth, Jacob lived his early years under the influence of a domineering and scheming mother; he seems to appear in a little better light when his own individuality comes into play. Thus, the story of Jacob's life should not be looked upon as an account of God's blessing on wickedness but rather as an account of God's patient dealing with a sinful man until he became Israel, "fighter for God."

The Misplaced Blessing (27:1-46)

It was customary for a Hebrew patriarch to bestow an oral blessing on his children prior to his death. That practice was characteristic not only of the Hebrews but also of at least some Semites of northern Mesopotamia. In an essentially nonliterate society, oral transactions were extremely important; and the oral blessing had the force of a legally-binding oral will, as texts from the Mesopotamian city of Nuzi demonstrate. The binding character of the blessing is clear because Esau did not argue for a transfer of the blessing to him just because a mistake had been made. He merely asked for some additional blessing.

Isaac's Plan to Bless Esau (27:1-4). Isaac was old and blind and perhaps in rather poor health, for he feared imminent death. How old he was may be computed from the age of Jacob. Stigers argues that Jacob was 77 at the time of the oral blessing.[1] Since Isaac was 60 when Jacob was born (25:26), it is necessary to add 60 to 77 to get the age of Isaac. At 137 he may have felt about ready to pass on, but he was destined to last for additional decades—until the age of 180 (35:28).

Isaac determined to bestow the oral blessing on Esau, even though God had clearly designated Jacob as the heir of the covenant. It seems inconceivable that God's revelation to Rebekah had never been shared with Isaac. It is not so certain, however, that Isaac knew of Esau's sale of the birthright to Jacob. But he certainly did know of Esau's marriage to pagan wives and a lifestyle that did not fit him to be the son of promise. It is incredible that the patriarch could so flagrantly fly in the face of divine ordination and arrange for the consummation of a misplaced oral blessing. As has been suggested, perhaps he needed the stimulation of Esau's best hunting and culinary efforts to fortify him for the procedure. Esau shared blame with his father in agreeing to go ahead with the plan even though he had given his oath to transfer the birthright to Jacob (25:33).

Rebekah's Plot to Deceive (27:5-17). But Rebekah and Jacob were at fault, too. Without a prayer to God to intervene or remon-

strate with Isaac, they concocted a plan to deceive the patriarch.
Rebekah was the instigator and Jacob her pliant accomplice.
Rebekah overruled Jacob's questions and objections. She solved
the problem of smell by dressing Jacob in Esau's clothes to provide
the odor associated with his hunting, and the problem of his hairy
skin by covering Jacob's neck and arms with goat hair. The fact
that Rebekah and Jacob were in line with God's sovereign plan
did not excuse their actions. It is not justifiable to do evil that
good may come of it. And both Rebekah and Jacob were to suffer
greatly for their sin. Great strife immediately entered the household. Rebekah was destined never again to see the apple of her
eye, upon whom she had lavished so much affection. Jacob was
forced into exile where he would suffer twenty long years of deceit
and domination of Laban. That Rebekah and Jacob should ever
have thought of deceiving Isaac shows something of his weakness
as a person and as a leader of the family, as well as weakness in
their own character.

Isaac's Blessing on Jacob (27:18-29). When Jacob was ready to
present himself to his father, immediately Isaac was suspicious.
Hardly had there been time to hunt for game and dress it and cook
it; the voice was Jacob's. The explanation that God had prospered
him and so shortened the time was no assurance to Isaac, because
Esau was not given to dropping pious phrases. The feel of Jacob's
hairy goatskin covering and the smell of his hunter's clothing
helped to assure the patriarch, however; and he was ready to
bestow the blessing. The contents of the blessing include: (1) a
vision of fruitfulness and plenty; (2) rule over other peoples of
the earth (to be fulfilled during the days of the Hebrew empire
and especially during the Millennium); (3) headship in the family ("master over your brothers"); (4) and promise of protection
("bless those who bless you"). The latter is a reiteration of a
major feature of the Abrahamic Covenant: treatment of the descendants of Abraham would be a basis of judgment of peoples
of the earth.

Esau's Remorse and Plea (27:30-41). When Jacob had "scarcely
gone out" from the presence of Isaac, Esau arrived from hunting.
Soon he had dressed his game and prepared it for his father. In
startled tones Isaac asked, "Who are you?" Equally surprised,
Esau answered, "I am Esau." Why should he not be surprised?

He had done exactly what his father had instructed him to do. Then Isaac "violently shook all over" and gasped out what must have been a rhetorical question, "Who then is he . . .?" Immediately he sensed what had happened and said, "Blessed shall he be." That was not merely a wish or a refusal to transfer the blessing but a recognition of the fulfillment of God's sovereign purposes in the life of Jacob.

Then Esau broke into loud sobs and begged for a blessing too. Though Isaac acknowledged Jacob's deception, he knew the situation could not be changed. As Hebrews observes, "He [Esau] could bring about no change of mind" in his father (Heb. 12:17, NIV). In response, Esau bitterly assailed his brother, "Is he not rightly called Jacob; twice he has deceived me." Continuing to sob, Esau again begged his father for a blessing. Isaac said in effect, "I have made him your master and blessed him with plenty, what else is there?" But when Esau pressed further, Isaac said, "Away from the fertile places of earth shall your dwelling be, and away from the dew of heaven"—an apt reference to the mountain fastnesses of Edom where little rain falls. His descendants would be warriors ("live by the sword") and would be subject to the Jews ("your brother will you serve"). But there would be times when the Edomites would gain freedom from the Hebrews. The pattern of subjugation and freedom may be observed in such passages as 1 Samuel 14:47; 2 Samuel 8; 1 Kings 9:22; and 2 Kings 14:7. For his humiliation before Jacob, Esau bore a grudge against him and determined to kill him after his father passed away.

Rebekah's Reaction (27:42-46)

When Rebekah heard of Esau's determination to get revenge, she decided to take action to protect Jacob. Either she did not know of Esau's plan to wait until after the death of Isaac to kill Jacob, or she believed the death of Isaac to be imminent. If it occurred to her to seek Isaac's help in restraining Esau, that point is not raised. She wanted to be sure that Jacob was safe; so she urged him to flee to her brother Laban until Esau's anger cooled. The "few days" she thought would elapse lengthened into twenty years and Rebekah never saw her favorite again. "Bereft of both of you in one day" must refer to the potential murder of Jacob and

Esau's banishment or execution for the crime. But of course Rebekah could not send Jacob away on her own accord in a patriarchal society. And she wanted him properly despatched rather than to have him flee for his life. Therefore she approached Isaac about sending Jacob away on an honorable mission: to get a wife from among her people as Isaac had done. It was about time; he was 77. In the process of the conversation, the degree of grief caused Esau's parents by his godless wives comes clear. Discreetly, Rebekah said nothing about Esau's threats on Jacob's life.

Jacob's Journey to Haran (28:1-22)

His departure (28:1-9). It is not strange that Isaac should accede to the wishes of Rebekah. Certainly he did not know what a large part she had had in the deception used in gaining the oral blessing and therefore was not prompted to be especially angry with her. Though piqued with Jacob, he recognized God's preference for him and the fact that he needed a wife in order to fulfill the promises of the covenant. Moreover, he knew that sons of the covenant should not be unequally yoked with pagan women of Palestine. That principle had been operative in the choice of a wife for him, and it should apply to his efforts on behalf of his sons as well. And of course he understood that it would be wise to separate Jacob and Esau for a while.

So Isaac called Jacob and sent him on his way. Jacob was not to marry a pagan Canaanite but to go to Paddan-aram (probably meaning "field of Aram"), the area in northwestern Mesopotamia where Haran was located (cf. Gen. 25:20) and there find a daughter of Laban, his mother's brother. The purpose for going there was not to keep the bloodline pure but to find a woman with spiritual ideals. Jacob was to leave quickly: the imperatives "up, go" ("go at once," NIV) indicate urgency. El Shaddai (God Almighty), the God of omnipotent power, will prosper Jacob on his way. Isaac was very much aware of Jacob's place as heir of the Abrahamic Covenant because his blessing referred to numerous descendants for Jacob who would some day possess the land of Canaan, which had been promised to Abraham.

As Jacob left on his journey, the sacred historian interrupted the narrative to comment on how Esau had responded to recent events. Recognizing how upset his parents were over his marriage

to Hittite wives, and how determined they were to have Jacob
avoid Canaanite entanglements, he took a third wife who was a
descendant of Abraham through Ishmael. In so doing he failed to
improve his standing with either his parents or with God, for
Ishmael was not in the line of promise.

His dream (28:10-15). As Jacob made his way northward, he
stopped for the night in the vicinity of what is now Bethel. Located about forty-five miles in a straight line north of Beersheba,
the spot must have taken three or four days to reach as he trudged
over the hills without the benefit of a good road. As darkness
overtook him, he propped his head on a stone and fell asleep.
There he lay, alone, defenseless, and with an uncertain future.
Perhaps he tossed in troubled sleep. In his extremity God met
him, as He often meets us when we come to the end of ourselves.

Jacob had a dream in which he saw a ladder with angels ascending and descending upon it. The ladder portrays the constant
contact that exists between earth and heaven, and the angels are
God's messengers (*angel* means "messenger") that present human
needs to God and bring God's help in return. It is significant that
Jesus applied that symbolism to Himself as "the way" to God or
the mediator between heaven and earth (John 1:51; cf. John 14:6;
1 Tim. 2:5). But instead of merely working through His agents,
in this instance God Himself "stood" above the ladder. The attention of heaven was focused on the one who was to father the progenitors of the twelve tribes of Israel and who was in a sense to
launch the fulfillment of the Abrahamic Covenant.

"I am Yahweh." God Himself spoke to Jacob. That was the
first of seven divine appearances to the patriarch (see 31:3; 32:1-
2; 24-30; 35:1, 9-13; 46:1-4). What God said included a broad
reiteration of the Abrahamic Covenant to Jacob: (1) promise of
the land of Canaan; (2) innumerable descendants; and (3) blessing of all peoples through his seed (the Messiah). But it also
included important personal guarantees: (1) provision and protection for Jacob; (2) his return from Mesopotamia. What more
could the lonely wanderer ask?

His consecration of Bethel (28:16-22). When Jacob awoke, he
was overwhelmed at what he had seen. He had stood at the very
"gate of heaven," and his vision of God had filled him with reverential fear. Such a vision goes a long way toward the making of

the man of God (cf. Isa. 6). Contemporary Christians often are too busy comparing themselves with each other and therefore are rather satisfied with the result; a vision of God stirs one to worship, reveals shortcomings, and leads to life-changing decisions.

Having met God in that place, Jacob called it *Bethel* ("house of God"). Evidently Bethel was located near the town of Luz and in time gave its name to the town. Also, Jacob turned up on end the slab on which he had rested his head to serve as a memorial pillar of the momentous event that had occurred there, and he anointed it with oil. Such memorials and their consecration were common in Hebrew experience (Lev. 8:10-11; Deut. 27:1-8). Later, when the Hebrews were tempted or ensnared by Canaanite cultic practices (including "standing stones"), they were forbidden to erect such pillars (Lev. 26:1). There was no animistic motive involved in Jacob's action, as sometimes has been charged; he merely sought to commemorate an event. Moreover, there is no basis for the claim that Jacob went to that place because it was a cult center where he might obtain some sort of assurance for his needy soul. It was merely a place near a town where a weary shepherd happened to sleep, and it became a worship center at a later time.

Verses 20-22 should not be construed as cheap bargaining but rather as a vow of gratitude. Verse 20 legitimately may be translated "Since God will be with me." He accepted God's promise and committed himself to returning to God a tenth of all He would bestow (a second reference to the voluntary tithe, cf. Gen. 14:20). Jacob was not postponing a decision to accept and serve God until God had made good on His promises.

Jacob's Sojourn in Laban's Household (29:1—30:43)

Jacob's Meeting with Rachel (29:1-14). Fortified by the promise of God, Jacob's steps were lighter as he continued his journey to the northeast. After some three weeks on the road he knew he was nearing his destination, so he stopped to make an inquiry. The scene was and still is common in that region: flocks of sheep and their shepherds gathered around a well (a well with stored water, equivalent to a cistern). Jacob soon learned that the shepherds were from Haran, that Laban was alive and well, and that his daughter Rachel was just arriving with a flock of his sheep. While she came nearer, he had a chance to get an answer to another question. Why did these shepherds wait near the well while the sun was high in the sky? Why didn't they water the sheep and put them out to graze some more? That question reflects Jacob's aggressive spirit and his desire to take advantage of opportunities for advancement. The explanation was that it was necessary for several shepherds to gather in order to lift the heavy stone from the well; possibly they were young boys who could not remove it singly. Or they may have made an agreement to water their flocks together for some other reason.

At that point Rachel arrived and Jacob removed the stone from the well and watered her flock without waiting for other shepherds to arrive. In that action both his strength and his impetuosity are revealed. Then, overcome with the emotion of the moment as he realized he had successfully and happily completed his arduous journey of some 400 miles, he "kissed Rachel and wept aloud." When she was told who he was, she left the sheep with him and ran to tell her father. Laban was excited too and ran to the well to meet Jacob. He greeted him in true oriental style and accepted him as his own flesh and blood. The son of Laban's sister, who had left home ninety-seven years earlier, Jacob was naturally welcomed.

Jacob's Marriage (29:15-30). Jacob was sincerely received into Laban's family—he joined them at meals and benefitted from what sleeping accommodations could be offered him. He did not loll around the house, however, but worked at whatever chores needed to be performed. Days went by, and at length a whole month had passed, during which Jacob worked according to that informal arrangement. Finally Laban sought a more formal wage agreement. What Jacob really wanted from Laban was the hand of his younger and more beautiful daughter Rachel, whom he had come to love very much, but for whom he was unable to give a dowry price. In a moment of impetuosity and yearning for Rachel, Jacob might have made Laban an offer he could hardly refuse; or Laban could have pressured Jacob to accept a demanding labor contract. The text does not elucidate how the agreement was made. It only reports on the terms: seven years of work as Rachel's bride price. Evidently at that time Laban had only two daughters and no sons; that explains why Rachel served as a shepherdess.

That Rachel was more beautiful than her older sister is clear, but it is not so clear that there was anything wrong with Leah. The RSV and NIV state that she had "weak eyes," and some commentators conclude that she had poor vision. But the Hebrew original may just as easily be construed to mean that she had pale eyes, instead of the dark, flashing eyes orientals often prefer.

The years flew by. Jacob's love for Rachel was so great that the period seemed only "a few days." But when the seven years were up, he demanded his wife. Laban appeared to acquiesce, making a great marriage feast and bringing his veiled daughter Leah to Jacob instead of Rachel. The deceiver had been deceived! He had met more than his match in Laban. Actually Laban had never fully committed himself to giving Rachel to Jacob, as the evasive language of verse 19 reveals. And in verse 21 Jacob had only asked for his wife—not Rachel by name. Laban weakly tried to clear himself by hiding behind the local custom that an elder sister should be married first, which perhaps was true but should have been stated earlier. Then the crafty old patriarch offered to give Jacob Rachel too—for another seven years of labor. But this time Jacob would not have to wait seven additional years; he could marry Rachel at the end of the customary week of wedding festivities (cf. Judg. 14:17), evidently without any further ceremony or celebration. Jacob was powerless to resist Laban's demands and capitulated to the inevitable. Mosaic law later prohibited marriage to sisters at the same time (Lev. 18:18), and at least one reason why appears in the subsequent unhappy relationship between Leah and Rachel.

Since the 1940s, when the Hurrian texts from Nuzi in northern Mesopotamia began to make an impact on biblical studies, it has been increasingly common to view the Jacob-Laban narrative in its Hurrian context. Thus, if a man (Laban) found himself without a male heir, he might adopt someone as his son (Jacob) and might seal the agreement with the marriage of a daughter (Leah, Rachel) to the adopted one. The adopted son had a responsibility to care for his adoptive father in advanced age and to provide him with a proper funeral. In the event that the adopter subsequently had natural sons (as evidently happened in this case), the adopted heir lost headship in the family and most of his inheritance rights. In a somewhat unrelated detail, when a Hurrian woman was married,

frequently she was given a servant girl (Zilpah, Bilhah) who not
merely waited on her but might bear children for her husband in
the event she was unable to do so. Such children became legal
children in the household and heirs of the estate.

Jacob's Children (29:31–30:24). In reading this passage, it is
easy to get lost in a mere listing of the births of children and to
lose the significance of what it has to say. First, after more than a
century and a half when there was only one heir to the Abrahamic
Covenant at a time, the more numerous progeny promised Abraham finally begins to appear on the scene. Second, nearly all the
progenitors of the twelve tribes of Israel emerge in this brief
passage. Third, the evils of polygamy and the strife it may produce
become abundantly clear. Fourth, Jacob's intense love for Rachel
and the preferential treatment shown her does not seem to jibe
with God's choice; He honored Leah and her handmaid with eight
sons to the four borne by Rachel and her handmaid. Moreover,
Leah's son Judah and his descendants became the head tribe; and
the descendants of her son Levi provided the priesthood. By way
of contrast, the tribes of Ephraim, Manasseh, and Benjamin (from
Rachel's line) did not come off very well in history. Fifth, God's
denial to Jacob of more sons by Rachel may be viewed as punishment or at least discipline for his sinfulness. Sixth, Jacob's partiality and his general handling of his family led to strife and
mother groupings that were to affect the history of Israel for centuries thereafter.

All the eleven sons mentioned here seemingly were born between Jacob's seventh year in Haran and his fourteenth year, when
he sought to leave. It is not possible, therefore, that all of these
children came consecutively; some must have been concurrent. Of
the number, Leah gave birth to six, her handmaid Zilpah to two;
Rachel bore one and her handmaid two. In addition, daughters
were born. Dinah is the only one mentioned by name here; perhaps she came along later (see v. 21; note also Gen. 37:35). The
names given to the sons are expressions condensed into proper
names and indicate the hopes associated with their birth and the
divisions and tensions of the household.

The passage opens with Leah trying very hard to win the affection of her husband. Yahweh saw she was "ill-regarded" or
"slighted" or "not loved." The word may mean "hated," but that

is certainly too strong here. It may be, however, that sometimes Jacob was downright difficult with her. God prospered her with a son whom she called *Reuben* (meaning "look, a son") because "Yahweh has looked on my misery." Probably the following year she bore *Simeon* ("hearing"), so called because "Yahweh has heard that I am not loved." Probably the year after that she gave birth to a third son and named him *Levi* ("attachment" or "joining") because she hoped Jacob would become attached to her now that she had presented him with three healthy sons. Perhaps for the fourth year in a row Leah gave birth to a son and this time called him *Judah* ("praised") because she gave great praise to God. When evaluating the character of Leah, it is significant to note that in three of those four births her faith focused especially on God. Her spiritual perception or orientation befitted her as a mother in the line of promise.

Meanwhile, probably by the time Simeon was born, Rachel had become inordinately jealous of Leah and extremely impatient to have a child of her own. As she pouted and fussed, Jacob became angry with her and reminded her that it was in God's (Elohim, the creator God's) power and will alone to give offspring. "Withheld from you"; Jacob did not of course speculate that Rachel's inability to bear children may have been punishment leveled against him. Nor was he able to comfort his wife; nor did he make an appeal to God on her behalf as his father Isaac had done. So Rachel sought her own expedient and Jacob acquiesced. Her maidservant Bilhah bore Jacob a son who was called *Dan* ("vindicated") because she thought God had vindicated her. Then Bilhah gave birth to a second son whom Rachel called *Naphtali* ("wrestling") because in the wrestling or rivalry with her sister she had won. But the Hebrew indicates the wrestling or struggle was also with God.

When Leah saw that she had temporarily ceased bearing children, she also resorted to the expedient of giving her handmaid to Jacob. Her action seems quite unjustified, but perhaps the rivalry of the sisters for the affection of their husband was so intense that she decided to have additional children in that way. Zilpah gave birth to *Gad* ("good fortune") and *Asher* ("happy").

When little Reuben was about four years old, he went out in the field one day during wheat harvest. The yellow berries of the mandrake caught his eye, and he picked some and brought them to his mother. When Rachel saw the "love-apples," to which popular superstition accorded the power to promote fertility, she asked for some. Relations were so tense in the household that Leah exploded. Rachel had stolen her husband's affections; now she wanted her son's mandrakes also. Evidently Leah's sons had not yet won for her Jacob's affection. The sisters bargained— Rachel got the mandrakes (with no results) and Leah the right to Jacob for the night (with the result that she bore a fifth son, *Issachar*, meaning "reward"). Again the effects of bigamy are evident: shameless bargaining of the sisters for their husband and Jacob's being shuttled back and forth between wives and their handmaids. Probably the following year Leah bore Jacob a sixth son and called him *Zebulun* ("bridegroom's gift") because now "my husband will bring me gifts."[2]

At last, near the end of the second seven years that Jacob served for Rachel, Rachel bore him a son. Jacob must have been about 91 at the time. In humility, Rachel gave God the glory for taking away her reproach; and in faith she named the child *Joseph* ("may he add") because her hope was, "may the Lord add to me another son" (NIV).

Jacob's New Wage Agreement (30:25-43). Jacob's fourteen years of service to Laban were over. He wanted to be released from his labor agreement and permitted to return home. And in a patriarchal society it was necessary for the patriarch to release all those wives and children, which were technically members of Laban's household. As he prepared to go, Jacob called attention to the quality of his labor. Then Laban proceeded to bargain with Jacob in an effort to retain his services. First he recognized Yahweh's blessing on him for Jacob's sake, which he claimed to have learned by divination—but could have seen by simple observation. One needs to be careful about labeling Laban as a rank idolator on the basis of this passage and later events, but he seemed to have little real faith in or knowledge of God. Then Laban made a very generous offer, "Name your wages, and I will pay them."

As Jacob proceeded to negotiate, he frankly reminded Laban that Laban had very little wealth before Jacob's arrival and that that wealth had expanded tremendously under his careful management. "Yahweh has blessed you at my every step"; your greater wealth today has resulted not only from my good efforts but also especially from the blessing of God. He said in effect, "I have served you faithfully, but when am I to provide for my own household?" If Jacob were to leave Laban at that point, he would have been without the means of supporting his large family enroute, or in Canaan on return.

The proposal made to Laban was very generous. Generally sheep were white and goats black or dark brown. Jacob suggested that in the future he be given all animals of deviant colors as pay for his labor: speckled or spotted or dark colored sheep and speckled or spotted goats. Presumably these would be a small minority and Laban would get the better of the bargain. Moreover, Jacob proposed that all animals presently of deviant color be removed from the flocks and herds so as not to increase his opportunity of breeding to his advantage. Laban agreed to that arrangement and immediately separated his animals according to color, putting those of deviant color in the care of his sons and separating them by a three-day journey. Evidently he did not trust Jacob and wanted to make it impossible to use sheep and goats of the separated herd for breeding purposes.

Then Jacob appears to have engaged in subterfuge to gain control of Laban's livestock. He cut shoots from poplar, almond, and plane trees and peeled away the bark in strips so as to expose the white inner wood. Then he put those branches in the watering troughs so they would be in front of the animals as they came to drink and to mate; the result was that a substantial number of the young had deviant coloration. In addition, he engaged in selective breeding (vv. 40-42). Thus in a very brief time Jacob's flocks and herds grew rapidly, and he had to employ servants to care for them and to purchase camels and donkeys for use in animal control and transportation to grazing grounds.

The question immediately arises as to whether that means of producing off-colored animals was biologically possible. And there is a moral or ethical question of whether God should have blessed trickery to enable Jacob to make off with Laban's livestock. Modern zoologists generally agree that a visual experience of that sort during conception or pregnancy could not affect the embryo. And it has been suggested that Jacob, who had been working with animals for most of a century, knew his animal husbandry well and would not have been taken in by a groundless superstition. Perhaps all he intended to do with the branches was to provide an aphrodisiac with the sight, or chemical substance in the water, in order to promote conception. To be sure, Laban would benefit most by such a plan, but Jacob would also benefit.[3] This passage makes it crystal clear that Jacob's success resulted not from subterfuge (and thus he did not support an old wives' tale) but selective breeding (30:40-42) and the blessing of God. Jacob himself gave full credit to God for the kind of variegation on the pelts of newborn animals (31:10-12).

In fact, as more and more of Laban's livestock passed to Jacob, Laban sought to change the ground rules; each time he did, the coloration of the newborn changed in Jacob's favor (31:8-9). Certainly no human devices could manage that. In passing, it should be noted that the genes capable of producing those various colorations had to be present in the parent animals; they were then concentrated differently in their offspring to give rise to the coloring that appeared.

NOTES

1. Harold G. Stigers, A Commentary on Genesis (Grand Rapids: Zondervan, 1976), p. 211.
2. Derek Kidner, Genesis (Downers Grove, Ill.: Inter-Varsity, 1967), p. 162.
3. For a discussion of this biological question and Jacob's actions see Henry M. Morris, The Genesis Record (Grand Rapids: Baker, 1976), pp. 474-76; J. B. Haitsma, The Supplanter Undeceived (Grand Rapids: Haitsma, 1941); and the comments on Genesis 31 in this book.

11

JACOB (2)
FLIGHT AND SETTLEMENT IN CANAAN

GENESIS 31:1–36:43

Jacob's Flight (31:1-21)

Jacob's situation had greatly changed sociologically, personally, and economically from what it had been twenty years before, or even six years before. Sociologically, when he came to Haran presumably he had been adopted into Laban's family and had become his heir. Now natural sons of Laban were on the scene and entitled to most of his estate. Personally, he had wives, a family, and a means of supporting himself. Economically, he had become quite well-to-do and had rapidly siphoned off Laban's wealth—legally, according to contractual arrangement. As Laban's sons saw the major part of their estate passing into Jacob's hands, they began to get ugly. And the increasing animosity Laban had for Jacob could not be hidden; it was written all over his face. Those uncongenial circumstances tended to encourage Jacob to leave. And since he had obtained in Haran all he could ever hope to get, there was no reason for him to stay. God ordered him to go back to Canaan and promised, "I will be with you"—important as he sought to tear away from Laban, make the trip home, and face the confrontation with Esau.

Fearing a nasty scene with Laban and perhaps an effort to stop him from leaving, Jacob made plans to leave secretly. He called Rachel and Leah for a conference out to where he was watching the flocks. There he rehearsed the change in their father's attitude, his faithfulness in labor for Laban, Laban's efforts to cheat him, and God's gracious provision in giving him Laban's livestock. "Ten times" is probably not to be taken literally but in the fashion of a modern American's exclamation that something has happened a dozen times. Much of what Jacob had to say his wives knew;

118

perhaps he had kept some of it pent up until this time. Probably his relation of the dream was new information to them. The way Jacob began his comments about it is instructive: "In breeding season I once had a dream" (NIV). It would seem that he had had the dream some years earlier; perhaps it was the dream that prompted him to make the bargain with Laban six years earlier and even to try his hand with the peeled branches. Verses 4-12 seem to be parenthetical. Verses 3 and 13 talk about leaving. The command to leave "at once" (v. 13) could not have been part of an earlier dream; it clearly applied to the present moment.

The reply of Rachel and Leah indicates the degree of their estrangement from their father. The way things were going they had no further hope of any inheritance from him. Laban now had sons to inherit the family estate; Jacob, their husband, had been cut off and they had too. Then came out the bitterness that had rankled in their breasts for years. They had been treated as foreign slaves in the household and had, in effect, been sold for all Laban could get out of the deal. Then instead of using part of the dowry provided by the groom for their benefit, as was customary, Laban had used it in his economic ventures. Much of that wealth God had now taken from Laban and given to Jacob; that wealth they felt rightly "belongs to us and our children." Therefore they believed they were doing nothing wrong in taking what was rightly theirs and that in view of the estrangement that had taken place, they should go.

Preparations to leave went forward rapidly. There was no fear of detection because Laban was some distance away attending to the spring sheep shearing. Jacob put his family on camels (probably for greater speed, if necessary), drove his livestock ahead of him, and also took along "all the goods he had acquired by purchase" while in Paddan-aram. The latter demonstrates that Jacob also had become something of a trader; whether he put those belongings on pack animals or on wagons is not stated. With Laban out of the house, it was easy for Rachel to carry off her father's household gods (*teraphim*, v. 19), unknown to Jacob. Why she did so is a matter of some debate. Perhaps she was still given to idolatry. Possibly she wanted them as amulets that would provide continued fertility. But the Nuzi texts cast her actions in a different light. According to Hurrian custom, posses-

sion of the household gods carried with them inheritance rights
and symbolized headship of the family. Perhaps that is what
Rachel wanted for Jacob. The fact that they bore great significance in that family situation is indicated by the fuss Laban made
over them. If they were merely figurines used in worship, he could
have obtained more.

Laban's Pursuit (31:22-43)

While Jacob traveled south as fast as he could, events moved
as rapidly in Laban's household. How soon Jacob's escape was
discovered is not known; but when it was, a messenger was dis-
patched and found Laban on the third day after Jacob left. No
doubt Laban raced home and organized the pursuit party immediately. Why he should have especially missed the teraphim is
not clear, unless he took a quick inventory of what was missing
before starting out. Or possibly he sought to pray before them for
blessing on his journey. Jacob must have had a four- or five-day
head start on Laban; but with no herds to slow him down, Laban
was able to travel much faster and he caught up in seven days of
hard riding, presumably by camel. Laban assumed that Jacob
took the main route to Canaan; and if he had any doubts about
which way Jacob had gone, he could check periodically with shepherds or farmers along the way. A group of Jacob's size could not
travel secretly. At length he caught up with Jacob in Gilead, east
of the Jordan. But before he did God appeared to Laban in a
dream, warning him to say nothing "good or bad" to Jacob—
neither to try to persuade him to return nor to harass him.

As Laban met Jacob, he put on a blustering act of righteous
indignation and hypocrisy. In fleeing secretly, Jacob had denied
him the privilege of saying good-bye to his dear loved ones and
of giving them a proper farewell. Though bringing no specific
charges of wrongdoing on Jacob's part, Laban declared he had the
power to harm him. Then, as an anticlimax to his bombast, Laban
declared that God had forbidden him to harm Jacob and implied
that therefore he would not. "The God of your fathers" indicates
that Yahweh was not Laban's god, but of course Laban was afraid
of any supernatural power. Then Laban concluded by claiming
to understand why Jacob should want to return to his kinfolk,
but demanded an explanation of why Jacob should steal his gods.

Now it was Jacob's turn to speak. His first statement was brief and straightforward. He frankly admitted his leaving by stealth because of the fear that Laban would try to take away his daughters from Jacob. Then he made a rash commitment that if Laban's gods were found in the possession of any of his people, that one should be put to death. And he invited Laban to search all his stuff in the presence of the relatives he had brought along and to take away any stolen goods he might locate. Laban accepted the invitation and went from tent to tent searching everything thoroughly. The tension heightened as he came into the last tent—Rachel's. He "felt all over the tent" without success while Rachel sat on her camel's saddle, in which she had hidden the teraphim. She professed to be in great misery with menstruation and unable to get up. The deception of father and husband had rubbed off on her! Laban went away disappointed.

As the search continued Jacob became increasingly angry. When it was over, his pent-up emotions erupted in a defense of his conduct and service in Laban's household. First he challenged Laban to produce any of his belongings found in the search of Jacob's baggage. Then he spoke of his careful oversight of Laban's flocks: so meticulous that he had suffered no losses through miscarriage at the birth of lambs and goats. He observed that he had been forced to make good losses suffered through attacks of wild animals or theft. He suffered much from heat by day and cold by night as he fulfilled his duties, and often lost sleep in his exercise of watchfulness. He was scrupulously honest in the conduct of his labor. He endured many salary alterations and would have returned home empty-handed if God had not intervened. Finally Jacob asserted that God had seen his hardships and the injustices he had suffered at the hands of Laban, "and He rebuked you last night."

Laban's response to Jacob's speech was to avoid the question of his treatment of Jacob and the quality of Jacob's service. Instead he talked about his rights and his likelihood of vengeance. Speaking as a patriarch, he laid claim to his larger family and all the goods that belonged to them, irrespective of the labor contracts made with Jacob. He tried to put the best face possible on the existing situation. Speaking as a father, he implied that he could not possibly harm his daughters. But he knew he could not reclaim what he was losing nor avenge himself for his loss because God had warned him against either course of action; so he called for a covenant.

The Covenant Between Jacob and Laban (31:44-55)

This covenant also might be called a nonaggression pact. Laban's main purpose in proposing it was to restrain Jacob from any retaliation in the future if he should become very rich and powerful in Canaan and/or if the teraphim should surface and Jacob should try to lay claim to his estate. Jacob was quite content to make such an agreement; he had no intention of going to Mesopotamia again, and he was glad to put the tensions of recent years behind him.

Jacob found an oblong stone and set it up on end as a pillar, to serve as a witness and a memorial of the event and possibly as something of a boundary stone between them. Then they gathered stones and heaped them around the pillar to serve as a rude table on which they ate a covenant meal together to seal their agreement. The heap of stones was meant to be a "heap of witness" or a testimonial to their pact; both Aramaic (*Jegar Sahadutha*) and Hebrew (*Galeed*) names for the heap are recorded. A third name, *Mizpah,* meaning "lookout point," was also attached because Laban considered it to be a place where Yahweh could stand watch to prevent them from going against each other. And Laban called on the gods of the respective parties to help keep the treaty.

When Laban finished his rather long statement about the covenant, Jacob swore to it by the "Fear" of his "father Isaac," his designation for Yahweh. That reference seemed to hark back to the reverential fear of God and the total dedication to Him experienced by Isaac on Mount Moriah. He swore to the covenant by the sovereign God, obedience to whom may demand life itself. It is almost amusing to contemplate the pleasant sentiments presently associated with Mizpah and the parting benediction, "The Lord watch between me and thee, when we are absent one from another" (KJV), when one thinks of the threatening implications involved in their origin. Presumably the parley and covenant consumed a day. After a night's sleep, Laban was ready to depart. As he bade farewell, he kissed his daughters and grandchildren and gave them his blessing, recognizing that they now belonged to Jacob. Though no reconciliation had been achieved, at least a proper parting had been effected.

Preparation to Meet Esau (32:1-32)

As Jacob took leave of Laban and journeyed south, he stood at the entrance of the promised land. There "angels of God drew near to him" or encountered him. Though evidently always present as "ministering spirits" (Heb. 1:14), now they made their presence known to Jacob in some way. How they revealed themselves is not stated, nor is it clear whether anyone else saw them; presumably they did not. That appearance assured Jacob of divine watchcare and was a tremendous encouragement to him as he faced an uncertain future, including an irate brother. He called the place *Mahanaim* ("double camp" or "two hosts"), for he had seen angelic hosts arranged alongside his people.

Jacob's first order of business was to make his peace with Esau, so he sent an advance party to make contact with his brother. "To the region of Edom" indicates the direction Jacob's messengers went; by this time Esau had settled in the mountain fastnesses of Edom east and south of the Dead Sea. Jacob's message to Esau was diplomatic, showing deference to his brother ("master . . . servant"). He stated frankly where he had been and that he had been "detained"; otherwise he might have come much sooner. Then he gave some indication of his present economic status, either to show that he sought no charity from Esau or that he had no designs on Esau's share of the family estate. He only sought Esau's favor, however; he did not beg forgiveness for any wrongdoing. Jacob's messengers came back with the alarming news that Esau had four hundred men with him, and they brought no reply. Evidently Esau wanted to size up things for himself before responding. Why Esau had so many men under his command can only be guessed; perhaps he was engaged in some marauding expedition or had plans for expanding his territorial holdings. It seems highly unlikely that he would have put together such a force to subdue Jacob when fifty or one hundred would have been adequate for such a venture. Exercising the prudence often practiced by caravans in the East, frightened

Jacob divided his company into two sections, so if the one were attacked the other might escape.

Then Jacob went to prayer. His prayer is a model in many ways. First, he rested on the word of God. In this case he put himself in covenant relationship. God had made a covenant with Abraham and confirmed it to Isaac and Jacob. Certainly He would make good on His covenant promises. Moreover, He had specifically directed Jacob to return to Canaan and committed Himself to do good to him there. Second, Jacob presented himself as unworthy of God's goodness to him. Third, he made a specific, pointed, urgent request for deliverance. Fourth, he returned to the word of God with its promises; the long-range fulfillment seemed to take some of the pressure off the moment.

Next Jacob developed a plan for meeting Esau. Often commentators criticize him for doing so, as if he were always scheming. But it is clear that his confidence was really in God, and God does not expect us to sit on our hands and do nothing when faced with an emergency. He determined to send a substantial gift to placate his brother: a total of 580 animals divided into five groups. The number gives some small clue as to Jacob's total wealth at that time. As each drove reached Esau with the explanation that it was a gift from Jacob for Esau, hopefully the effect would be cumulative. Jacob sent them on ahead with their attendants, and moved all his own possessions and family across the ford of the Jabbok River; he was left on the north bank alone.

But he was not destined to sleep. Through the night a man wrestled with Jacob. The man, the Angel of Yahweh (see Hos. 12:4-5), evidently was a preincarnate appearance of Christ Himself. Though the wrestling was physical, it symbolized a spiritual struggle between Jacob and God to determine whether Jacob in self-will and self-reliance and guile was to manage his own affairs or whether he was to bow completely to God's management of his life. Jacob put up a powerful struggle until God dislocated his ball-and-socket joint and rendered him incapable of continuing the struggle. Unable to fight longer, Jacob merely hung on tenaciously to receive a blessing from the "man" whose divine character he gradually came to recognize and whose power over his life he came to accept. Then God changed his name from *Jacob* ("supplanter") to *Israel* (not "prince with God," KJV; but "fighter

for God" or possibly "may God strive [for him]"). The pronouncement, "You have struggled with God and with men and have overcome" (v. 27, NIV), does not mean that Jacob had defeated God.
Rather in his struggles with God he had capitulated and thus had
won His blessing. Moreover, that blessing of God included victory
over human opposition. Since protection against the vengeance
of Laban had occurred already, that reference especially must
have concerned Esau. After all, the meeting with Esau was his
most weighty problem at the moment. In commemoration of that
event Jacob called the place *Peniel* ("face of God") because he
had seen God face to face there. Further reminders were his dislocated hip and the refusal by Israelites henceforth to eat that part
of an animal.

Meeting with Esau (33:1-16)

At last the dramatic moment arrived. There was Esau's company on the horizon! Jacob's approach to the situation was con-
siderably altered from that of the previous evening. Instead of
dividing his family into two camps (the one possibly being sacrificed for the benefit of the other), he arranged them according to
maternal groupings, putting the dearest in the rear. Then Jacob
courageously walked unarmed before them to meet Esau, bowing
himself in sevenfold obeisance to his brother, recognizing him as
an elder and superior. Thus he threw himself on Esau's mercy.
As Jacob had won God's blessing in capitulating to Him; so now
he was to win reconciliation to Esau by capitulating to him, by
taking the place of the younger and inferior son. Then Esau's
heart melted and he hugged and kissed Jacob in acceptance. At
length Esau noticed Jacob's family and they too bowed in humble
obeisance. Finally Esau referred to Jacob's gift, which he considered quite unnecessary because he had "much." But Jacob made
it clear that acceptance of the gift would be evidence of Esau's
acceptance of Jacob's good will toward him and an indication that
reconciliation was complete.

"Seeing your face is like seeing the face of God" was not idle
flattery. On the surface it seems to mean that the change in Esau's
attitude toward him was evidence of God's working in Esau's life
and on Jacob's behalf. But it may have a deeper meaning: as
Jacob had seen God's face at Peniel and the encounter had

changed his attitude and relationship toward Him, so the encounter had altered his attitude toward Esau. Viewed in that light, the gift was designed not merely to change Esau but also evidenced a change in Jacob and revealed his contrition and goodwill. Esau felt compelled to accept the gift, and Jacob was relieved.

Then Esau urged departure southward. He had a large company of men to support, and presumably wanted to finish the business he was on when he met Jacob. Jacob thought it unwise that they travel together. Some have taken that as evidence of Jacob's mistrust of Esau and his men, but that is not necessarily so. It is not unreasonable to take Jacob's statement at face value. He had driven his animals and his family about as fast as he could to escape Laban. Now they needed to go at a slower pace, whereas Esau's men would be impatient to travel much more rapidly. Jacob's children were very young; the oldest was about twelve. And Jacob did not want or need an armed escort. He was depending on God for protection, and he did not seek armed confrontations with people of the land. So "on that day," the one on which the reconciliation took place, Esau started south toward Seir (Edom).

The fact that no visit of Jacob to Seir is recorded, or that there is no reference to Jacob's having gone to see Isaac, does not mean that none occurred. It is not the purpose of Scripture to provide a complete biography of anyone or a complete history of anything. The sketchy nature of Jacob's biography is immediately evident.

Jacob in the Promised Land (33:17—35:29)

Sojourn at Succoth (33:17). Presumably Jacob found it impracticable to move his family and his flocks and herds very far at all for a while. He settled down at Succoth, just north of where the Jabbok flows into the Jordan, and built a house for himself and booths or shelters (Hebrew, *succoth*) for his cattle. That he stayed there for several years is determined from the fact that Dinah would have been a child of not more than five or so when she arrived at Succoth, but she was a girl of marriageable age when the family moved to Shechem. Moreover, Joseph was about six when the family reached Succoth and seventeen shortly after the events at Shechem (37:2).

Tragedy at Shechem (33:18–34:31). Jacob's next major move brought him to Shechem. Since the point is made that now he had arrived safely in Canaan from Paddan-aram, probably it is to be assumed that he had not been moving around in Canaan (visiting Isaac, etc.) before that time. Why Jacob did not go directly to Bethel on return to Canaan in order to express his thanks to God for all He had done is not clear (see Gen. 28:20-22). The stop at Succoth did nothing for him; the period at Shechem was disastrous. Though God did not specifically command Jacob to return to Bethel, He did instruct him to go back to Canaan (31:3, 13); so at least the years spent at Succoth, outside the land, were lived in disobedience. Conceivably the tragedy at Shechem might have been avoided if Jacob, and especially his growing family, had been refurbished spiritually at Bethel soon after return to Canaan. At Shechem Jacob bought a piece of land from Hamor, the father of Shechem, perhaps symbolizing his expectation of eventual control of the land. On that parcel Joseph was to be buried, and his traditional tomb is shown there today. The fact that Jacob could part with one hundred pieces of silver shows something of his growing wealth and may indicate commercial as well as pastoral activities. At Shechem he built an altar to God, Who he called *El-Elohe-Israel* ("mighty is the God of Israel").

But in settling down too comfortably among the Canaanites, Jacob encouraged among his children a carelessness in attitude toward them. Dinah evidently began to socialize with Canaanite women, and apparently Jacob did nothing to stop her. In the morally loose Canaanite society, unattached women were fair game for the young men of the community. Soon Shechem, a Hivite prince, raped Dinah, who may have been about fourteen at the time. Whether she encouraged his advances or willingly submitted to them is not noted. But Shechem's action did not turn out to be a mere sexual conquest; he "loved the girl" and sought to marry her. And evidently she remained at his house until the conclusion of the grisly affair (v. 26). Shechem then urged his father to arrange for his marriage to the young woman; parents made such arrangements in those days.

News travels fast in a small town. Jacob heard about what had happened rather promptly; but his sons by Leah, the full brothers of Dinah, were out in the fields and inaccessible for the moment.

The custom of the day required that those brothers act in concert with their father in making decisions concerning the family; he could not act alone. Hamor "went out" to Jacob, to his home outside the city. At length Dinah's brothers came in from the field and heard the whole story; they were "grieved and infuriated" over the affront to Israel—the sense of their distinctness from the Canaanites was evident. That distinctness in orientation is underscored as Shechem and Hamor showed no evidence of chagrin or wrong in what had happened. They proposed a marriage alliance between Jacob's family and the people of the land. "The land lies open to you"; unclaimed territory was still available here and there. Then Shechem seemed to wish to mollify all with a sufficient financial settlement: "Set high the bride price [to be paid to the parents] and the gift [presented to the bride]."

The sons of Jacob must have had at least a brief private conference, out of which came a stratagem. They would propose circumcision for all the males of Shechem, who then would appear to be like the Hebrews, as a condition for a marriage alliance. Jacob could go along with that because to him their participation in the rite signified conversion; though he seemed not to ask how long it might take for the Hebrews, the smaller group, to be completely engulfed in Canaanite paganism. Shechem and Hamor could agree because to many Canaanites it was only a marriage rite anyway, and it seemed a cheap price to pay for advantages to be gained. The sons of Jacob could agree because of planned retaliation to be revealed. Evidently Jacob had no inkling of their designs.

The agreement needed to be ratified by the men of the village, and a conference was held at the gate of the city—the official gathering place. Hamor and Shechem sold the community on the benefits of the agreement by observing that as they became one people, all of Jacob's considerable wealth would belong to the people of the town. So the males of Shechem submitted themselves to circumcision. On the third day, when the men of Shechem were especially incapacitated, Simeon and Levi (evidently with their servants) took swords and slew all the males of the town, including Shechem and Hamor, and snatched their sister from the house of Shechem. The other sons of Jacob evidently had had no part in the massacre, but they were perfectly willing to participate in the general and thorough plundering of the village, presumably keeping the wives and children as slaves. All of this was done by people of God as people of God in the process of avenging immorality!

Moreover, in taking advantage of the weakness of the males, they had broken a sacred covenant, honorably agreed upon. And it is incredible to observe that Jacob's expostulation with Simeon and Levi referred not to the heinousness of their crime but to the fact that now Jacob's family was in trouble with the inhabitants of the land and might be destroyed by them. His weak rebuke deserved an equally weak defense from the brothers: "Should our sister be treated like a prostitute?" But Jacob had the final word on the conduct of Simeon and Levi on his deathbed (49:5-7).

Reaffirmation at Bethel (35:1-15). At that crucial moment God spoke to Jacob (how is not stated), commanding him to return to Bethel. The reason was at least twofold; his family was in physical danger and needed somewhere else to go, and spiritual and moral conditions among the family had reached such a low ebb that a reformation was imperative. "Go up" to Bethel does not mean to go north because it was located twenty miles south of Shechem. The primary reference must be to the higher altitude of Bethel (about 1,000 feet above where he was), but a hint of a higher spiritual plane also may be implied. "Tarry there" must be the true intent of the command; he was to build an altar and meet God, not to take up residence. The words "God Who appeared to you" would remind Jacob of his revolutionary experience some thirty years earlier and his unfulfilled vow. "When you fled" is being repeated; before it was flight from Esau, now from the Canaanites.

Jacob obeyed but he knew that more than simple change of location was required. They must all prepare to meet God. He who would stand in the holy place must have "clean hands and a pure heart" (Psalm 24:4). Jacob, as the priest of his larger patriarchal family, launched a major clean-up campaign. "Discard the foreign gods"; objects of devotion to another god must go first, whether Rachel's teraphim if she still had them, the idols of the servants who had come along from Haran, or Canaanite gods of Shechemites who may have been retained as slaves. "Purify yourselves" may involve ceremonial washing but must have referred primarily to purging of the heart. "Change your clothes" involved proper respect for the occasion and symbolized putting off the old and putting on the new (cf. Eph. 4:22-24; Col. 3:9-10). All responded to Jacob's command and gave him their idols and even earrings that had idolatrous connotations (perhaps serving as amulets); certainly this did not involve a surrender of all jewelry. Why Jacob buried that idolatrous collection instead of burning or otherwise destroying it is not clear; perhaps it was a less emotional means of disposal.

Having prepared themselves to meet God, Jacob's family departed for Bethel. The "terror of God," a supernatural fear of molesting the Hebrews, fell on the villagers they passed. So they arrived safely at their destination, and Jacob built the altar he had been directed to construct and called the place *El Bethel* ("God of Bethel"). The God of Bethel, not just a local cultic deity, but the God of Abraham and Isaac, the true God who had so generously watched over Jacob, now appeared to him again. In language and content very similar to Genesis 28:13-15, God reaffirmed Jacob's change of name and the details of the Abrahamic Covenant. And Jacob for his part reaffirmed his earlier naming of the place as Bethel. Such an act had wider significance at that time; only Jacob knew of the name before, now his whole family was apprised of it. Likewise his whole family observed his erection of the memorial pillar and its consecration.

At Bethel Deborah, Rebekah's nurse, died and was buried under an oak, which was called *Allon Bacuth* ("oak of weeping"). That aged and devoted family servant must have been 170 or more at the time. How she happened to be in Jacob's entourage can only be guessed. Possibly messengers had informed Jacob of his mother's death at some point and Deborah had come along.

Death of Rachel and Birth of Benjamin (35:16-29). Shortly after the repeated promise that Jacob would have a numerous progeny, the account is given of the birth of his twelfth son. While the family was moving south from Bethel, probably on the way to Hebron or Beersheba, Rachel died in childbirth. Before she expired, she realized she was giving birth to a son whom she called *Benoni* ("son of my sorrow") but whom Jacob renamed *Benjamin* ("son of my right hand," signifying an honored position). That sad note helps to explain Jacob's particular affection for Benjamin.

The death of Rachel took place on the way to Ephrath (Bethlehem) but "some distance" from it (v. 16). Jacob decided to bury her along the way instead of taking her body to the family burial place in the cave of Machpelah. Probably her tomb was actually located near Jerusalem (Migdal-eder, v. 21, likely on the outskirts of Jerusalem; cf. 1 Sam. 10:2; Jer. 31:15) six miles north of Bethlehem. The traditional tomb of Rachel, about two miles north of Bethlehem, seems to be too far south to have any claim to validity.

Events at Bethel may have sent Jacob's family in a new direction, but they did not eradicate the corrupt tendencies of the sons. Soon after the spiritual high at Bethel, Reuben committed incest with Bilhah, handmaid of Rachel. But now that Rachel had died, Bilhah was called a concubine of Israel. Instead of exhibiting conduct becoming a son of Israel, Reuben showed something of the moral weakness of Jacob's sons. Why Jacob did not come down hard on Reuben at that time is not clear, but he later took from him the birthright during the oral blessing (Gen. 49:4).

The birth of Benjamin provided a reason for a complete listing of Jacob's sons. They are grouped according to their mothers: Leah first as elder sister, then Rachel, and then the handmaids or concubines. These all are said to have been born to Jacob while in Paddan-aram, though of course Benjamin was not. Perhaps that discrepancy is eliminated by including in the Paddan-aram period of Jacob's life the entire time he was absent from Isaac. His return to his father at Hebron is recorded in the very next verse. The listing of Jacob's sons, the death of Isaac, and the record of Esau's descendants ties up loose ends and prepares the reader for emphasis on Jacob's sons during the rest of the book. Actually Jacob's return to Isaac did not occur just before Isaac's death. Careful computation shows that Jacob lived near Isaac for some ten to twelve years before Isaac died at 180.[1] Thus Isaac still would have been around to witness Jacob's grief over the presumed loss of Joseph.

The Descendants of Esau (36:1-43)

In describing Esau's descendants, the sacred historian seeks first to dispose of the collateral line of Esau before proceeding with the main line of promise, and second to show that the promise of a land and people to Esau was fulfilled (Gen. 25:23; 27:39-

40). The detail in the outline provided here is justified by the continuing relationship between the nations of Edom and Israel. Several observations on this chapter are in order. (1) When the names of Esau's wives (vv. 2-3) are compared with those of Genesis 26:34 and 28:9, certain differences appear. Those may be accounted for by the fact that a person could have more than one name, name changes were fairly common, and the use of names was fairly fluid in oriental custom. (2) The five sons of Esau's three wives appear the same in verses 4 and 5 and in 1 Chronicles 1:35. (3) The time of Esau's move to Edom or Seir (vv. 6-8) is somewhat debated. A few would place it after the death of Isaac, by which time the property of both was considerable; but most would place it earlier. It is to be noted that when Jacob sought to make contact with Esau on return to Canaan, he sent messengers in the direction of Edom (32:3); and as Esau returned south, Jacob promised to join him in Edom (33:14). Yet that move refers to the brothers' numerous livestock, which would not have been possessed at an earlier time. Perhaps what really happened is that Esau did move away much earlier, possibly soon after his marriage to pagan wives, and that reference here is to a formal separation occurring soon after the death of Isaac.

(4) The increase of Esau's sons into a people is described in terms of grandsons, tribes, tribal chiefs, and kings. Among the ten grandsons of Esau (vv. 9-14), of special interest is Amalek, evidently the father of the Amalekites. As later enemies of the Israelites the Amalekites attacked them in the wilderness (Exodus 17:8-16) and were therefore ordered destroyed by Samuel (1 Sam. 15:2-3). The fact that a "country of the Amalekites" is mentioned already in Genesis 14:7 may be accounted for either in the sense of a country where the Amalekites later would live or a tribe into which the sons of Esau may have married and eventually came to lead. Also of interest is the conjunction of Eliphaz and Teman in verses 11 and 15. Events of the book of Job therefore would seem to have taken place in Edom (see Job 2:11; 15:10-11). After noting the chiefs of the sons of Esau (vv. 15-19), the text proceeds to comment on the inhabitants of Edom whom Esau found there when he entered—the sons of Seir the Horite (vv. 20-30). There were twenty chiefs among them as compared with only thirteen among the descendants of Esau. Esau moved in on them and de-

stroyed them and appropriated their land (Deut. 2:12), but probably there was also intermarriage with them. Subsequently eight kings are mentioned as ruling in Edom before any king rose in Israel. Since none of those was described as having descended from a royal father, either the elective principle or force must have been employed. The reference to kings in Israel (v. 31) does not demonstrate a late date for composition of this passage because Moses himself anticipated the coming of kingship to Israel and indicated what kind of person a king should be (Deut. 17:14-20). All the reference need imply is that kings had not yet risen in Israel. The lack of recognizable town ruins and the extremely poor knowledge of the historical geography of Edom makes it virtually impossible even to speculate intelligently on the location of place names or tribal sites mentioned in this chapter.

NOTES

1. See Harold G. Stigers, *A Commentary on Genesis* (Grand Rapids: Zondervan, 1976), p. 265.

12

JOSEPH (1)
EARLY LIFE TO EXALTATION IN EGYPT

GENESIS 37:1–41:57

Some think of Joseph as a dreamer, but he had only two recorded dreams, and they were not a result of some psychological aberration but a revelation from God himself. Others think of him as a proud and unwise young man who lorded it over his brothers. He may have been imprudent in telling his brothers his dreams, but there is no indication he did so in a haughty fashion or that he was otherwise inordinately proud. If he did sometimes act superior to them, it could well have been because of his father's favoritism. In fact, Joseph was a victim of his father's favoritism; his brothers "hated him" for it (37:4).

The Genesis account presents Joseph as a very unusual young man, possessed of a strong or sterling character, of a high morality and fidelity to God and his superiors. He was also characterized by gentleness in human relations. Remarkably, Joseph's spiritual and moral strength does not appear to be based on or related to God's periodic and direct revelations, as was true of Jacob, Isaac, and Abraham. Presumably, then, Jacob must have put a lot of character-building truth into the young man's life at an early time, for it does not appear that he could have obtained such information from any other source. If that is the case, Jacob did a much better job with Joseph than with his other sons.

It is customary to treat the final chapters of Genesis as an account of the life of Joseph, and so they are. But, more importantly, they are a narrative of God's faithfulness in preserving the Hebrews, the line of Jacob. The connection is clear: "This is the history of Jacob. When Joseph was seventeen . . ." (v. 2). God intends to tell the story of Jacob's later years and the preservation of his family, but He uses Joseph to accomplish His purposes. The last chapters of Genesis exude the sovereignty and tender watch-care of God.

Causes of Animosity Against Joseph (37:1-11)

In capsule form the reasons for the rift between Joseph and his brothers are spelled out. (1) He incurred the wrath of the four sons of the handmaidens Bilhah and Zilpah by exposing some of their failures on the job (v. 2). (2) He faced the continuing animosity of all his brothers because of Jacob's evident favoritism for Joseph. That reached its climax in Jacob's bestowal of a special robe on Joseph. It was not a "coat of many colors," but exactly what it looked like is unknown. Certainly it was ostentatious and was designed to be a status robe (a similar robe was worn by princesses in 2 Sam. 13:18). Commonly it is thought to signify that in presenting it Jacob was designating Joseph as his chief heir and successor. Naturally that would upset all his older brothers.

(3) Joseph clinched the opposition to him by reporting God's preference for him as revealed in two dreams. In the first of the dreams his brothers were subservient to him and in the second, his mother and father and brothers. The interpretation of both dreams was clear to Joseph, his brothers, and his father. As someone has observed, Old Testament personages never needed interpreters to explain their dreams; their message could be plainly understood. Sometimes, however, they did need to interpret the dreams of pagans (e.g., Pharaoh, Nebuchadnezzar). Generally "mother" is made to refer to Leah, but some would rearrange events to have this occur before Rachel's death. If Rachel were still alive, however, it would seem that her reaction to Joseph's supposed death later on would be recorded. Verse 11 indicates responses to Joseph's dreams: increased jealousy of his brothers, while Jacob "retained in his memory" those things after a rebuke for Joseph.

Joseph's Sale into Slavery (37:12-36)

Ultimately the brothers had their chance for revenge. With the exhaustion of grazing lands farther south, they had moved their father's flocks to Shechem, some fifty miles to the north of Hebron. In the process they had been gone so long that Jacob became concerned for them and sent Joseph to inquire about their safety. When Joseph got to Shechem, he learned that his brothers had moved some twenty miles farther north, to Dothan. As Joseph appeared on the horizon the brothers were infuriated. Here was their father's favorite in his splendid robe, no doubt come to supervise them. Why should he stay at home anyway while they bore the heat of day and cold of night watching after the livestock?

"Here comes that dreamer!" Clearly they resented his superior position in the family and now plotted to destroy him to prevent God's purposes from coming to fruition. Apparently Reuben was not a party to the plot; and when he learned of it he tried to foil it. Not only did he seem to have been more generous than the others, but as the eldest he also had some responsibility for the others. He suggested that they not kill Joseph but merely throw him in a cistern, one of the artificially prepared water cisterns in the area. It was his plan to free Joseph later.

When Joseph came up to them, they stripped him of his robe and threw him into a dry cistern, where he could be expected to perish. Evidently Joseph begged so passionately for his life that the wrenching scene left an indelible impression on their minds. Years later in Egypt they referred to it (Gen. 42:21). After such a scene the brothers in callousness of heart sat down and ate.

At that point a caravan came by; the main route from Damascus through Gilead passed by there on the way to Egypt. One of the principal commodities in the trade with Egypt was spices. Judah, also now wishing to avoid bloodshed and the associated guilt, suggested selling Joseph into slavery in Egypt. This they did for twenty pieces of silver, the stated price of a slave in the early second millennium B.C. The terms Ishmaelites and Midianites are both applied to the members of the caravan. Though they are somewhat interchangeable, Ishmaelite is the more inclusive term and Midianite the more restricted of the two. Midianites were part of the larger Ishmaelite grouping (see Judg. 8:24).

While all that was going on, Reuben had separated himself from the others, either to do necessary chores or eventually to find his way to Joseph's place of confinement undetected in order to release him. When he reached the cistern he found Joseph missing. In great anguish he cried, "Where can I go?" How could he face his father; he as the eldest had some responsibility for the younger ones. Presumably Reuben then helped the others stain Joseph's coat with goat's blood to show to their father. On seeing it, Jacob went into mourning for his supposedly deceased son. He who had deceived his own father with a goat skin and had obtained thereby the oral blessing now was deceived by his sons with the blood of a goat. All the efforts of Jacob's sons, daughters, and probably daughters-in-law to comfort him were of no avail.

Judah and Tamar (38:1-30)

Though the account of Judah and Tamar is a parenthesis in the main line of the narrative, it fits here chronologically and serves several purposes. (1) It accounts for the three families of the tribe of Judah (Num. 26:20). (2) It helps to establish the validity of the levirate law (that a man should marry a deceased brother's widow to preserve his line, Deut. 25:5-10). (3) It demonstrates the contrast in the faith and chastity of Judah and Joseph under similar circumstances of temptation. (4) It shows the likelihood of future Hebrew liaisons with Canaanite women and the ultimate absorption of the Hebrews by the Canaanites if they remained in Palestine. Thus that distinctive people of God would have passed off the scene and the Abrahamic Covenant would have become null and void. Therefore a temporary move from Canaan into the separate district of Goshen in Egypt would help to further God's purposes for the Hebrews and the world.

(5) It contributes to our knowledge of the ancestry of David and of Christ (Pharez or Perez was an ancestor of Christ, Matt. 1:2). It demonstrates further the degree to which the humanity He came to save is tainted by sin. Moreover, the introduction of Tamar, a Gentile, into the line of Christ suggests the universal aspect of the redemption He came to offer. It is useful to observe once more that Scripture does not varnish over the weaknesses of the human beings God chose to use.

"At that time," the time when Joseph was sold into Egypt, Judah "departed" or "went down from his brothers," perhaps in a falling out over the Joseph affair; it is not said that "he left his father." "He pitched his tent in company with" (NEB) a man from Adullam, a place thirteen miles southwest of Bethlehem, which was to figure in the history of David (1 Sam. 22:1; 2 Sam. 23:13). Here he rather easily took up with a Canaanite woman, quite in contrast to what he and his brothers would permit to happen to Dinah at Shechem. From that union three sons were born: Er, Onan, and Shelah.

Er was guilty of some unspecified wickedness and God slew him in judgment. Onan then half-heartedly went through the motions of levirate marriage; but *"whenever* he lay with his brothers' wife," he failed to consummate sexual union. Thus in his failure to perpetuate the line he committed an affront to the family, against Tamar, and against himself. For his repeated actions, God finally took him in judgment. Then Judah urged Tamar to remain a widow until Shelah was a little older and could marry her. But Judah feared that somehow Tamar was jinxed and that if she married Shelah, he too would die. Thus Judah would be without posterity. The years rolled by, and Shelah grew older but was never given to Tamar. In time Judah's wife died as well. Finally Tamar took things into her own hands. Removing her widow's clothes and dressing as a veiled temple prostitute, she lured Judah to have sexual relations with her. Her pay was to be a kid from his flock; but until he could deliver the kid, she demanded his personal seal and its cord, which he wore around his neck, and his staff. These would guarantee her safety in the event she became pregnant and was condemned to death for harlotry, and they proved Judah was the father of her children. Promptly thereafter Tamar put on her widow's clothes again and returned to her father's house. Thus it proved impossible for Judah to deliver the kid and reclaim his pledge.

Three months later Judah was told that Tamar was pregnant as a result of harlotry. As head of the family, Judah had to deal with the situation. Legally Tamar belonged to Shelah, even though Judah had not arranged for consummation of the marriage; so she could be considered guilty of adultery and worthy of death. At the moment of confrontation for her sin, Tamar produced Judah's signet and staff. He promptly admitted not only his complicity but also his greater sin in not giving Tamar to Shelah. After that incestuous relationship, it was proper that Judah have no further relations with Tamar (v. 26*b*).

Tamar gave birth to twins, whose struggle is somewhat reminiscent of that of Jacob and Esau. In the birth process *Zerah* ("scarlet") thrust out a hand first and had a scarlet thread tied on his wrist. But then he pulled his hand back and *Perez* ("breaking out") forced his way past Zerah. Perez, the more aggressive one, was actually the firstborn and became an ancestor of both David and Christ (Matt. 1:2). With the end of that episode, the stage is set for a need to move from Canaan and for comparison with the more exemplary life of Joseph.

Joseph in Potiphar's House (39:1-23)

As God continued to work out His sovereign purpose for the Hebrews, He led the Egyptian Potiphar to purchase Joseph as a slave. Potiphar was an "officer" of Pharaoh, king of Egypt. Potiphar's position is hard to identify; "captain of the guard" is considered to be an approximation, but "captain of the executioners" is also a possibility.

Yahweh blessed Joseph, and he was assigned not to prison duty or to the garden staff but to the household staff of Potiphar. There Potiphar had a chance to come to know Joseph as a Hebrew and servant of Yahweh; and Joseph's God-given talents of management became evident. Perhaps Potiphar concluded that God was with Joseph because he gave God the credit for his evident abilities; it is not clear how else Potiphar would have made such a determination. It does seem clear, however, that Joseph did not allow himself to become embittered by the treatment of his brothers; nor did he allow his spirit to be enslaved by captivity. He refused to be destroyed by circumstances. Perhaps the revelation received in his two dreams provided light regarding the ultimate outcome of things. As the blessing of God continued to rest on Joseph, Potiphar gave him more responsibility and finally made him chief steward, in control of all his property and his affairs. Then God evidently also blessed Potiphar for Joseph's sake.

God blessed not only Joseph's managerial skills but also his body. From a lad of seventeen he developed into a young man of twenty-three or twenty-four with a "handsome face" and a "good build." No doubt he often worked around the house in the topless, short kilt worn by Egyptians in the intense heat of their land. He increasingly appealed to the sensuous wife of Potiphar. So she began to try to seduce him; but he made it clear that he considered that betrayal of his master's trust to be a "great wrong" against him and a "sin against God." Thus he demonstrated both a great

140 GENESIS

loyalty to God and man, and he demonstrated conduct rooted in divinely-set standards. It is instructive to observe that Joseph met temptation by remembering that he belonged to God, by recognizing that capitulation would be defiance against God, and by avoiding the temptation as much as possible. Potiphar's wife kept pursuing him "day after day," but he refused not only her propositions but even to "be with her."

At last, one day when they were alone together in the house, she tried to force him, grabbing hold of the cloak worn around the shoulders either on cooler days or more formal occasions. Joseph fled without his cloak, not as a coward but to escape entrapment in immorality (2 Tim. 2:22). His conduct was just the opposite of Judah's in the previous chapter. The fury of the repulsed woman now led her to destroy what she could not have. Because she had Joseph's cloak, she was able to persuade both the other household servants and her husband of the truth of her allegations.

Joseph could have expected only death for such conduct, but either his excellent record of service or the fact that Potiphar did not fully believe his wife (possibly both) led to imprisonment instead. Again Joseph evidently refused to become embittered or destroyed by circumstances. His conduct commended him to the jailer. After a difficult initial period in jail, he came to sustain the same relationship to the jailer as to Potiphar, and for the same reason: "Yahweh was with him." Ultimately he became *de facto* warden in charge.

Important Contacts: Cupbearer and Baker (40:1-23)

In this chapter appears further indication of how God would work through Joseph to accomplish His purposes for the Hebrew people. First God had to get Joseph into Egypt; then He brought him into the home of an official (Potiphar) who apparently was not very close to Pharaoh. Through events in his household, God brought Joseph into prison where he came in contact with an official who had the ear of Pharaoh and through whom he would be raised to second in command of the entire realm.

Two high-ranking officials of the Egyptian court incurred the displeasure of Pharaoh (evidently on good grounds, as the Hebrew indicates) and were thrown into the prison where Joseph was incarcerated. These were such high-ranking officials that the "captain of the guard," possibly Potiphar, personally assigned Joseph to supervise them. The captain did that rather than merely leaving their care in the hands of the warden who had been favoring Joseph. If Potiphar was involved in that arrangement, evidently he had become impressed with Joseph's qualities all over again or had been led to distrust his wife increasingly (or both). And possibly the affairs of his household had declined notably since Joseph's incarceration.

In any case, Joseph had charge of the prisoners: the chief cupbearer and the chief baker. At least the former could be a very influential man at court. Of course he had to be a person who could be trusted implicitly. Among other things, it was his responsibility to see to it that the king's wine and food were not poisoned. He was in a position to discover and report plots on the king's life and to inform him about conditions in the realm and people who ought to be watched for managerial inadequacies or rewarded for abilities or achievements. He could become, in effect, chief confidant or right-hand man to the king. It is to be remembered that Nehemiah bore that relationship to King Artaxerxes of Persia.

After those men had been in prison for some time, each of them had a dream in the same night. The next morning Joseph who evidently was one who was not so overwhelmed with his own problems that he was unable to be attuned to the needs of others, spoke to them about their sadness. Both believed that dreams were a means of predicting the future, and they were upset because they were without an interpreter, one of the professional wisemen. Then Joseph magnanimously got involved. First he asked if it were not true that the God of heaven was the one who could give interpretations to dreams. Then, seeming to sense that he had got involved in this whole affair for some reason, asked about the character of the dream. In passing, it is to be kept in mind that there was no class or group of dream interpreters in Israel; the only two known interpreters were Joseph and Daniel, and they served pagan monarchs. The court officials decided to divulge their dreams. At the most they trusted the Hebrew and believed he might help them, at the minimum they really had nothing to lose. Furthermore, Joseph asked no fee for helping them and sought to strike no bargain.

First the cupbearer told his dream, which needs no elaboration. How Joseph knew its meaning is not clear, but presumably he withdrew and prayed for wisdom to interpret before presenting its message. In essence he reported that the chief cupbearer would be fully restored to his former post in three days. Only then did he ask a favor of the Egyptian: that the cupbearer speak to Pharaoh on Joseph's behalf to obtain his release from prison. Joseph reported that he had been "stolen," his word for being kidnapped, with a view to sale. "From the land of the Hebrews" may indicate that Joseph by faith had laid hold of the Abrahamic Covenant. After all, the Hebrews possessed very little of Canaan at that time, and the Egyptians would not have viewed the land as belonging to the Hebrews then. And without referring specifically to the problem with Potiphar's wife, he disclaimed any wrongdoing that should have landed him in jail.

Encouraged by the positive interpretation given to the chief cupbearer, the chief baker next described his dream. He had three baskets of "white baked goods" stacked on his head, the place where customarily they would have been carried in the Near East. In the top one was a variety of baked goods, specialties that the baker was able to create. And birds were eating them out of the basket and he was not able to drive them off. Joseph replied that again the three elements stood for three days; in three days Pharaoh would hang him and birds would eat his flesh.

It turned out just as Joseph had predicted. Three days later Pharaoh threw a birthday party, and as part of the celebration disposed of pending cases against various persons. Among them were the chief cupbearer, who was restored to his office, and the chief baker, who was hanged. But as often happens, in the excitement of his good fortune, the chief cupbearer forgot someone who had been a great encouragement in days of adversity—in this case, Joseph.

Pharaoh's Dreams (41:1-40)

After Joseph had spent two more years in prison Pharaoh had a dream. These must have seemed like very long years indeed as Joseph waited for rescue. But as someone has said, our stops as well as our steps are ordered by God. He was preparing a crisis, and He was preparing a leader for the crisis. His time clock was ticking away with absolute precision. At length Pharaoh had a dream. He was standing by the Nile watching the cows as he often must have done. Rarely would he have got very far from the Nile because the cultivated area of Egypt never was more than about ten miles wide in the Nile Valley. Often the cows stood in the water to cool off and sometimes came up to graze "among the reeds," reed grass or papyrus along the banks, not "in a meadow" (KJV); there were no meadows in Egypt as Americans or Europeans would know them. Pharaoh first saw seven fat and healthy cows come out of the river (source of all Egyptian life in an otherwise desert area) and then saw seven malnourished cows come out of the Nile and devour them. Then he woke up. Lapsing back into sleep, he had another dream with an agricultural motif. Egypt, breadbasket of the eastern Mediterranean, produced beautiful wheat and other grain on fields irrigated by the Nile. In this instance seven heads of grain were seen growing on a single stalk, followed by seven other heads of grain blasted by the scorching desert wind. The withered heads of grain consumed the healthy grain. Again Pharaoh awoke and was troubled by what he had seen.

Calling the "magicians" and "wisemen" of Egypt, the professional interpreters of dreams, he was disappointed by their inability or unwillingness to interpret his dreams. They may have guessed at least part of the meaning, but may have been afraid to present bad omens to Pharaoh. Then at the crucial moment, the chief cupbearer remembered Joseph and how he had interpreted the dreams for the two officials and how "things had turned out exactly as he interpreted" (NIV). Orders were sent to bring Joseph without delay; after waiting for so long, now he must hurry. But first he must be presentable to the king. Semites were bearded, but Egyptians smooth-shaven; Joseph shaved and probably was given a change of clothes to wear before Pharaoh.

The fact that the Genesis account records none of the usual obeisance required before an oriental monarch, and especially before Pharaoh who was regarded as divine and son of the sun god incarnate, is no indication that expected civilities were omitted. If Pharaoh had regarded Joseph as uncouth and incapable of functioning in the highest circles of government, he certainly would not have appointed him to second in command in the

realm. When Pharaoh gave recognition to Joseph's ability to interpret dreams, Joseph made it clear that God alone could provide
the meaning—not only could, but "would." With that assurance,
Pharaoh proceeded to rehearse his dreams for Joseph. The repetition was almost identical to the original telling except that this
time he said he had never seen such malnourished cows (v. 19)
and that even after they ate up the healthy cows, they were as
gaunt as before.

Joseph seemed to give an immediate interpretation; perhaps
God gave it as he heard the retelling of the dream. In the interpretation, Joseph subscribed to a high monotheism. There is no hint
of a murky concept of God, which is supposed to have existed
among the Hebrews at an early time and to have developed into a
full monotheism later. Moreover, Joseph did not merely report
what would happen, but what God was about to do (see vv. 25, 28,
32). God was in control of natural forces; in fact, He was assumed
to be superior to the god of the Nile and other Egyptian gods that
were supposed to guarantee fertility and prosperity. In essence,
Joseph said that the dreams were a unit. They foretold seven years
of plenty to be followed by seven years of famine, presumably to
be brought on by such a low Nile that there would not be enough
water for irrigation and by the blast of the eastern wind of the
desert, which would shrivel all growing things. Joseph further
declared that the reason for doubling the dream was to establish
the absolute certainty of those events and of their imminence.
Therefore Pharaoh should prepare for the future.

There is no hint that the famine was viewed as a judgment.
There was no condemnation connected with it, and seven good
years would precede it so preparation could be made to weather
the bad years. Joseph took the opportunity to add to the interpretation a friendly warning. Let Pharaoh find a good administra-
tor and an effective staff to launch a program of food storage. Store
twenty percent of the produce each of the seven good years so
there will be plenty during the years of famine, that the "land will
not perish."

The proposal pleased Pharaoh and his courtiers. Then Pharaoh
nominated Joseph before all his courtiers—all the inner circle of
the government—to take charge of the project he had just recommended. Pharaoh concluded that since the spirit of God was in

Joseph, and since God had revealed all that to him, evidently he had the ear of God and presumably therefore the wisdom to bring this task to completion effectively. Of course when Pharaoh spoke of God, his perspective was polytheistic, therefore that statement did not indicate a conversion to distinctive Hebrew monotheism. Although at this time the pharaoh was not the absolutist that he was during other periods of Egyptian history, apparently he found no opposition to his proposal. The powerful nobles who contested the absolute control of the central government probably would not have been at court anyway; likely they were off managing their own affairs.

Pharaoh then proceeded to install Joseph in his new position. Some have argued that that position was only supervisor of granaries, but this passage indicates more than that. Verse 40 says, "only in the throne will I be greater than you," and verse 43 refers to him as "second in command." Apparently, then, he was to be vizier or prime minister. Pharaoh first invested him with his signet ring, which was engraved and was used for the purpose of stamping soft materials (such as sealing wax) with the king's seal in order to give a document official status. Then he authorized him to wear the fine linen clothing of the nobility, put a gold chain or collar around his neck (as part of his symbols of authority), and authorized him to ride in the second chariot of the realm—which would be preceded by heralds ordering obeisance as he traveled about. His power would be so absolute that without his orders "no one will lift hand or foot in all Egypt."

Finally, Pharaoh gave him a new name and a wife. The name was *Zaphenath-paneah*, the exact meaning of which is uncertain; but one suggestion, "preserver of the living," might refer to his special function in Egypt—especially during the years of famine. His marriage to Asenath, daughter of the priest of On (later Heliopolis, just north of modern Cairo), should not be taken as an indication that he necessarily compromised his religious convictions. It is clear from the ensuing chapters that he remained faithful to the God of his fathers and to his Hebrew family ties.

Joseph was thirty years old when he took office in Egypt (v. 46). Since he came to Egypt at seventeen, he had spent thirteen years as slave and prisoner, probably seven or eight years as slave. During the seven years of plenty he faithfully stored food in the cities, establishing district collection centers (v. 48); probably he followed the twenty percent plan he had recommended to Pharaoh (v. 34). During the years of plenty, two sons were born to Joseph: *Manasseh* ("forgetting"), so named because God had made him forget his sorrows; and *Ephraim* ("fruitful") because God had made him fruitful in Egypt.

At the end of the seven years of abundance the famine set in as Joseph had predicted. "All lands" (vv. 54, 57) probably refers to the lands surrounding Egypt. The Sudan suffered with the reduced waters of the Nile, and Canaan suffered for lack of rainfall. When the people of Egypt cried to Pharaoh for food, he referred them to Joseph, who opened the granaries and began to sell what he had been buying for seven years. People from abroad began to come as well. Libyans and Asiatics could come by land and make purchases at the northern storehouses, and Sudanese or Nubians by water from the south.

13

JOSEPH (2)
FROM THE FIRST VISIT OF HIS
BROTHERS TO THEIR MIGRATION
TO EGYPT

GENESIS 42:1—47:12

First Journey of Joseph's Brothers (42:1-38)

The famine bit ever deeper in eastern Mediterranean lands. Canaan was among the areas hard hit. But word spread among the inhabitants there that food could be bought in Egypt, and a caravan of purchasers began to form in preparation for the southward trek (v. 5). At first, Jacob's sons seem merely to have sat around staring at each other helplessly. But finally, at Jacob's strong urging, they moved to join the others in buying food in Egypt. Jacob sent ten of his sons but kept Benjamin at home, fearing lest something should happen to him as it had to Joseph. And though Jacob had no proof of his sons' complicity in the loss of Joseph, he may have had some suspicions and did appear to hold them responsible for what had happened (see v. 36). Evidently Jacob had learned nothing about the evils of open favoritism and now put Benjamin on the pedestal once occupied by Joseph. Perhaps that fact rankled the older brothers' hearts as much as before.

At length the ten arrived in Egypt and appeared before Joseph to buy food. Certainly it was not necessary for Joseph to supervise all purchases of food, but probably he needed to be involved in decisions about how much food should be permitted to leave the country. And the group of Canaanites must have been large if the ten sons of Jacob were only a fraction of it. In the light of Joseph's first dream it is interesting to see his brothers prostrating themselves before him (v. 6), and his absolute control over the situation is underscored in the very strong Hebrew word for "governor." Joseph recognized his brothers, but they did not recognize him. It had been over twenty years since they had seen him (presently he was 37 to 40); now he was smooth-shaven and attired as an Egyptian, and he spoke to them through an interpreter (v. 23).

He "spoke to them roughly," not vindictively or spitefully, but in an effort to test and humble them and to bring about some major spiritual changes in them. That he was not merely trying to be nasty or pay them back for their treatment of him should be clear from such a passage as 45:5-8. Joseph decided to bait them with an accusation of being spies come to see the "nakedness"—defenseless, impoverished, and barren condition of the land. They declared they were not a reconnaissance force but sons of one man in Canaan on an errand to buy food. Their youngest brother and father were still in Canaan and the other brother was no longer living. Apparently they also commented on their families (v. 19). But Joseph continued to levy spy charges and demanded proof that they were not foreign agents. His first demand was that all of them be held as hostages while one of them returned to get the younger brother and prove the truth of their statements. To demonstrate that he meant business and to help bring about a change in their characters, Joseph threw them all in prison for three days. No doubt their servants were left in charge of their animals.

After the three days, Joseph indicated some relenting in his demands, because he feared God and was concerned for their starving households. So he decided to retain one hostage and let the others return with food for their families. But he warned them that without their youngest brother they would not see his (Joseph's) face again and would not even be permitted to live. At that point the ten suddenly became conscience-stricken and reached the conclusion that they were being put through this grilling because of their crime against Joseph, who had begged so urgently for his life (vv. 21-22). On hearing that, Joseph broke down and wept, but not so they could notice. Perhaps he did so because of the memory of his own suffering in earlier years, or because he saw some contrition in his brothers' hearts, or because he yearned so much to reveal himself to them and be done with the test. Then he took Simeon as hostage, the second eldest of the group, leaving Reuben as eldest to lead the company back to

Canaan and see to it that they all returned with Benjamin. In binding him before their eyes, he again reinforced the fact that he meant business and dramatized the fact that Simeon would remain in prison until they returned.

Then Joseph granted the request they had made days before and sold them the grain, but he put each man's purchase price back in one of his sacks. Presumably Joseph did not dip into the public till to give this money back to his brothers but paid for it himself because his steward later indicated that he had received payment for what they took (43:23). To return their money was an act of kindness, but it also was no doubt designed to fill them with consternation. In fact, when one of them discovered his money on the way home, they began to wonder what would happen to them and saw the hand of God in the developing circumstances. They really were frightened when later on at home they discovered that all of them had their money returned (v. 35). Parenthetically, it should be noted that that money was not coin but silver paid out by weight; coined money apparently did not originate until the first half of the first millennium B.C. in Lydia (western Asia Minor) as a result of trade contacts between Lydia and Greece.

When the nine returned to Jacob, they "told him all that had happened." There was no deceit or lying this time. They carefully rehearsed exactly what happened and told their father the truth. They might as well because Simeon's life was at stake and none of them would get any more food unless they could persuade Jacob to let Benjamin go back with them. Jacob's response was very self-oriented and again put Benjamin's line (Rachel's) on a higher level than that of Leah. It must not have been easy for the brothers to be informed once more that they were secondary in their father's affections. In spite of that fact, Reuben extravagantly offered the sacrifice of two of his sons (he had four at the time or soon thereafter, 46:9) if he failed to bring back Benjamin in safety. But Jacob brushed aside the offer and, for the present at least, was adamant about refusing to let Benjamin go. It is interesting to note that although Jacob had his heart set on elevating his descendants through Rachel, God chose to honor those coming through Leah instead. Judah's was to be the Davidic and messianic line. Often God's ways are very different from ours.

Second Journey of Joseph's Brothers (43:1-34)

The famine continued to be "severe in the land." Within a few months, no doubt, Jacob's family had "entirely eaten up" what his sons had purchased in Egypt. Seeking to evade the demand for Benjamin, Jacob urged his sons to return to Egypt to "buy a *bit* of food." They could not expect to get much; Egypt had to ration supplies carefully if all peoples of the region were to be preserved through the famine. But Judah reminded his father that "the man" was very firm; he would not see them again unless they brought their youngest brother. Seeking to avoid the inevitable, Jacob scolded them for needlessly volunteering information and continued to view the whole problem narrowly, as a threat to himself: "Why have you treated me so ill?" Then the brothers rehearsed once more in detail, openly and honestly, what had happened. They only had responded to questions and they could not have guessed that the Egyptian would have demanded to see Benjamin as evidence of their integrity.

Then Judah took the leadership again and reminded his father of the absolute necessity of sending Benjamin or they all would die of starvation; in fact, they had lingered too long already (v. 2, 10). Judah promised personally to "go bond" or "go surety" for Benjamin, and to do all in his power to guarantee his safe return. In effect he made himself responsible for Benjamin. Reuben's leadership (42:37) evidently had not been accepted because of his sin of incest; Simeon was in prison in Egypt; he and Levi bore the chief blame for the massacre at Shechem; so Judah was next in line to assume the leadership role. Reference to Benjamin as "the lad" or "the boy" does not mean that he was still a child; it simply designates him as the youngest of the twelve. He was twenty-one or older at the time.

Finally Jacob bowed to the inevitable. But he took every step to guarantee the outcome. First he arranged to send a gift for the governor, perhaps because protocol required it, or out of appreciation for the privilege of buying grain, or to placate his wrath as he had sought to assuage Esau's (32:13-21). During a famine the "best products" or "choice fruits" of the land would be meager, but he could send a "little" balm, gum, and myrrh—types of gum used especially for medicinal purposes and embalming—honey, pistachio nuts, and almonds. Second, he proposed open-

faced honesty in financial dealings: returning the money found in
their sacks and pleading a mistake in its being found there. Third,
he acquiesced to the demand for Benjamin's appearance. Fourth,
he prayed for God's blessing on the venture and resigned himself
to the will of God.

Joseph's brothers promptly went to Egypt, and when Joseph
saw them he ordered his chief steward to kill an animal and prepare a meal for them at noon. When Joseph's brothers learned
that they were being brought to his house, they were perplexed.
He had been so stern with them before that now they feared the
worst. They thought he was going to charge them with theft for
taking the money found in their grain sacks and that he would then
seek to enslave them. Before entering the house they tried to clear
themselves on that account with the chief steward. As they hur-
riedly whispered an explanation at the door, they greatly tele-
scoped the story, telling of the discovery of the money in their
grain sacks but not explaining that the discovery came in two
stages. The steward assured them that he had received their
money and everything was all right. His observation that God
had given them the treasure in their sacks does not sound like an
Egyptian's response; perhaps some of Joseph's piety had rubbed
off on him. That assurance was followed by Simeon's release.
Then with typical oriental courtesy, the steward provided water
for washing their tired and dusty feet and fed their donkeys. Having made themselves more presentable, the eleven got their gift
ready for Joseph. And in the process of handing it to him, they
bowed low before him twice (vv. 26, 28) in further fulfillment of
Joseph's first dream.

Joseph's questions put to the brothers about their father and
Benjamin must have made them very nervous, because they realized that it was impossible to tell where such questions would
lead. And they were "astonished" when they were seated in the
the order of their ages, from the eldest to the youngest. It was un-
canny that a foreigner could "divine" enough about them to do so;
he must have been supernaturally informed about their family
affairs. Joseph's meeting with Benjamin, whom he had not seen
since he was about a year old, was very touching indeed; and
Joseph finally lost his self-control—but not in their presence.
Joseph's comments about and to Benjamin were properly aloof

for a stranger, and the address of "son" was in order for one who was about twice his age and much above him in position.

The dining scene was properly Egyptian: Egyptians and Hebrews would not eat together, and a high official (especially of the priestly caste) would not eat with those below him in rank. Some have believed that that segregation between Egyptians and foreigners resulted from a social taboo, and others have concluded that it had a cultic basis, involving a belief that foreigners defiled the food. Since Egyptians opposed eating with Asiatics, it is assumed that a native Egyptian dynasty was in power when Joseph entered the land; if an Asiatic Hyksos dynasty were then in power, presumably that antipathy would have broken down. (See the subsequent discussion on the place of Joseph in Egyptian history.) During the meal Joseph tested his brothers further. He conferred greater honor on Benjamin than on the others, but his actions seem not to have stirred a ripple of resentment. They actually made merry with Joseph. Reformation was taking place!

Benjamin's Arrest (44:1-34)

Possibly Joseph entertained his brothers at dinner to be kind to them and to be with them. More likely, that act was a part of his greater strategy for bringing about their reformation. Unless they had access to his table, they could not be accused of taking his cup. Now Joseph was about to engineer the supreme moment of testing of his brothers. He commanded his chief steward to fill the men's sacks with all the grain they would hold and to put each one's silver in his sack as before; Joseph would not make his father pay for food. Then he was to put Joseph's silver drinking cup in Benjamin's sack. "And he did as Joseph told him" is an indication that the instructions were fully carried out. The steward did not merely cooperate with Joseph, as commentators sometimes suggest; he had no choice but to obey orders.

All this was done in the afternoon or evening so the eleven could be ready to leave for Canaan early in the morning. Soon after they left, Joseph sent his steward to catch up with them. When he did so, first he was to make a general accusation of wrongdoing and then to charge them with the theft of Joseph's silver drinking cup. The reference to divination connected with it is problematical. Some argue that since Joseph was without any kind of Scripture as a guide to life, it is natural to suppose that he practiced divination as those around him did. But the use of a divining cup in Egypt during that period is not otherwise known, and the practice was foreign to the Hebrews. It is entirely possible that Joseph did not engage in divination and that that was part of his pose, a means by which he claimed to know things about his brothers that they marveled at. Also, it has been suggested that the phrase can be translated "about this he would certainly have divined."[1] That is, such a theft perpetrated by them would not go undetected.

The steward found the brothers and leveled the charges as instructed, but all the brothers chimed in with denials of wrongdoing. To support their profession of honesty, they reminded him that they had brought back from Canaan the money they had found in their grain sacks after their first visit to Egypt. Then, so certain were they of their innocence, they declared that the one in whose possession it was found should be executed and all the rest would become "the man's" slaves. The second part of their declaration was significant; they were not willing to see one of their number punished by himself but professed a solidarity and a willingness of all to share in the blame. The steward returned to the test, announcing that only the one found to have the cup would become a slave; the rest would be free to go home. Parenthetically, it should be noted that classification of the theft of a silver goblet as a capital offense is not to be thought of as unduly severe. Down through history the poor commonly have paid dearly for stealing from the rich or public officials. Even in such enlightened lands as colonial America or eighteenth-century England, various relatively minor thefts were considered capital crimes.

Eager to prove their innocence, the brothers quickly lowered their sacks from their pack animals, and the steward began his search. Beginning with the eldest, he went down the line. As he passed from one to another, a sigh of relief went up over failure to find the cup. But tension also heightened. Would it be found among their grain? Finally it was found in Benjamin's sack, and they tore their clothes as they were convulsed with grief and consternation. They reloaded their grain and returned to the city to face Joseph.

With heavy footsteps and downcast eyes they entered Joseph's

house where he had waited for them. In abject humiliation they
fell on their faces before him. First he reproached them for their
ingratitude: "What . . . have you done?" Then he scored them
for thinking they could get away with such a thing with him who
had powers of divination: a reference to his actions of the day
before (and his divining cup), or to his reputation throughout
Egypt as interpreter of Pharaoh's dreams. Presumably he had
some inside track with God. In utter helplessness Judah stam-
mered out three questions: "What can we say?" "What can we
speak?" "How can we clear ourselves?" Then he declared, "Elohim [as judge rather than Yahweh as covenant-keeping God] has
uncovered the iniquity of your servants." Because they really did
not believe they were at fault in their actions in Egypt, the deeper
meaning of that reference must be that God had caught up with
them for their treatment of Joseph. Therefore, the mess they were
in was a result of divine retribution. Moreover, Judah emphasized
group solidarity: they were now all slaves to the governor of
Egypt. At that point Joseph tested them further, offering to set
them all free to return to their father except Benjamin.

His test brought forth one of the truly great speeches of history.
Judah's speech was great because of its sincerity of purpose, its
emotional depth, its altruistic concern, its revelation of the conversion of the speaker, and its substitutionary plea. To elaborate,
it was a very moving speech that presented the facts of the case
in a straightforward manner designed to win the mind of the governor to a release of Benjamin for the sake of their aged father.
The speaker, who once had not been concerned about causing
grief to his father, now put the aged man's interests first. In the
process he asked nothing for himself but now, as one who had
given bond to his father for Benjamin's safety, he offered to take
his brother's place in slavery in Egypt. Moreover, the speech was
great not only for its literary, psychological, and spiritual qualities, and its importance to the affairs of an obscure family thou-
sands of years ago, but also for its effects in the larger sweep of
history. It led to a reconciliation of Joseph and his brothers, the
preservation of the Hebrew people, and thus the preservation of
the line of the Messiah or Redeemer of all mankind.

One question remains, Was this the plea of Judah alone or did
his brothers agree? The answer was that they all had returned to

Joseph's house to support Benjamin. All of them had presumed themselves to be slaves to the governor because of the alleged theft. Judah included the others as part of the action at several points. They all clustered about as he spoke, and Judah declared that they all would be the cause of their father's death if Benjamin did not return (v. 31). They were in this together; a spirit of community had arisen among them. They had developed a spirit of true devotion to their father. Evidently a real change had come over them all. God had pursued them and revolutionized their hearts and had set their feet on a new and better path. They were ready for the next step.

Joseph's Revelation to His Brothers (45:1-15)

Not only were they ready for reconciliation with Joseph, but also he could restrain no longer the dammed up emotion that had been building for so long. Ordering all his servants out of the room, he revealed himself to his brothers, and the sluice gates of emotion were thrown open wide. No doubt Joseph cleared the room to give privacy for a purely family affair, to avoid embarrassment over any show of emotion that might occur, and to prevent the airing of ugly aspects of relationships of the people of God before unbelievers. In the process of his self-revelation Joseph wept so loud that his servants heard it. When ordered to leave, they would have retired at sufficient distance to allow his complete privacy. But servants never would remove themselves from their master at such a great distance that they could not hear his cry for help or his call to fulfill a command. The statement in 45:1-2 appears to be a summary: Joseph revealed himself to his brothers with great emotion, and the Egyptians heard about what was going on. The sense of verse 2 seems to be that Joseph's servants heard the emotional outburst and learned what occasioned it. Pharaoh's household also heard "about it," about the arrival of Joseph's brothers.

The next verses provide some elaboration of the summary. Aspects of the conversation included, first, Joseph's self-revelation to his brothers, at which "they were terrified," because they feared that the full weight of his judgment would now fall on them. Second, he sought to allay their fears by inquiring about things at home and inviting them to come closer and engage in intimate conversation. Third, he urged them not to continue to reproach themselves for what they had done to him; God in His sovereign purposes had used their evil actions for the good of the whole Hebrew cause. "Elohim sent me ahead" to "preserve for you a remnant," which otherwise might be swallowed up in a rapprochement with Canaanite culture, and "to save your lives," which are threatened by extinction in the great famine. As a matter of fact, five years of famine remained.

Fourth, he invited his father and all the rest of the clan to come to Egypt where he would provide for them. "Father to Pharaoh" was a title given to the vizier of Egypt and referred especially to his advisory function. Other aspects of his position and his honors are clear. The "region of Goshen" was in the eastern delta. A relatively uninhabited area, it lay open for Hebrew occupancy; and its grasslands would provide a grazing area for sheep and goats. There Hebrew sheep herders would not come in contact with Egyptian cattle raisers in the Nile Valley. In Goshen the Hebrews would have been very "near" Joseph if those events occurred during the Hyksos period when the capital was in the eastern delta, or fairly "near" him if those events occurred during the nineteenth century B.C. when the capital was in the Memphis area.

Fifth, Joseph embraced and kissed all his brothers, assuring them of his full forgiveness. Joseph was a truly great man. He bore no grudges and took the long look, fully recognizing how God had chosen to work in and through him. Sixth, the conversation included much more, perhaps details of life back in Canaan and of Joseph's suffering in Egypt (v. 15).

Pharaoh's Invitation to the Family (45:16-28)

Joseph had the power to care for his clan, but even a man of his stature ran the risk of jealousy on the part of other officials, or criticism of his actions—especially in a time when food supplies were so low. It was very important therefore to have Pharaoh enthusiastically concur with Joseph's instructions—and even to grant more than Joseph did: "You are commanded to . . . take some carts" to bring back the women and children. And "Never mind about your belongings" (NIV). In other words, "Don't bother to bring all your old half-worn stuff here; you may have the best of the land."

Of course Joseph followed the generous commands of Pharaoh, happily given because of all Joseph was doing for Egypt—and for him personally if the historical assessment suggested later is accurate. Then he added gifts of clothing for all and special gifts for his father and Benjamin. The parting admonition not to "quarrel on the way" was a comprehensive warning, which included the following: blaming each other for past actions, interpretation of Joseph's handling of them, and their response to favoritism to Benjamin.

When the eleven arrived in Canaan and told Jacob that Joseph was alive and was ruler of Egypt, "he was stunned" and refused to believe it. But gradually he was persuaded to change his mind, first by an oral review of Joseph's story and second by the evidence provided by the carts and the gifts. Presumably they made a full confession of their guilt in the treatment of their brother. Jacob's joy was fully restored: "My son . . . lives! I shall . . . see him!"

The Migration to Egypt (46:1-34)

It would appear from verse 1 that Jacob immediately and eagerly responded to the invitation from Egypt, in order to see Joseph and to enjoy abundant provision for his material needs. But closer observation leads to a somewhat different conclusion. He was, after all, living in the promised land, which had been given to Abraham and his descendants forever. In fact, God had intervened to prevent his father Isaac from going down into Egypt. Jacob apparently was troubled about removing from the place of promise. He started out from Hebron and traveled southwest to Beersheba. There, on the border of Canaan, he stopped to offer sacrifice to God and evidently to inquire of the "God of Isaac" about the advisability of the journey. God honored his cautious spirit and appeared to him there. "Elohim," the sovereign God who controls all affairs, told him not to fear the removal. In fact, in Egypt his descendants would not be absorbed into the local population but would multiply into "a great nation." Moreover, God promised to go with the Hebrews and bless them and to bring them back to Canaan again.

Comment is required on the phrase "bring you [singular] back" (v. 4). Certainly Jacob did not personally expect to return to Canaan alive. In fact, the last half of the verse clearly indicates that Jacob would die in Egypt. "Joseph's own hand will close your eyes" refers to the ritual of a son's respectful closing of his father's eyelids after death. Though the subsequent narrative records that Joseph buried his father in Canaan, and so his body returned, God's promise alluded to a continuing living presence. Therefore "you" must be viewed in a collective sense: "You," your seed, descendants, will come back again.

Armed with God's promises, Jacob fearlessly proceeded to lead the removal to Egypt. The text clearly says "all" Jacob's descendants went with him (v. 6) and then it specifically names them. Yet there are those who claim that later not all the Hebrews left Egypt during the Exodus because not all accompanied Jacob there. The names of the children and grandchildren are grouped according to each mother: those descended from Leah, 33; those descended from Zilpah, 16; those descended from Rachel, 14; those descended from Bilhah, 7—for a total of 70. Then the total of those who *accompanied* Jacob is given as 66, not counting the wives (v. 26). The difference of four is accounted for by subtracting Joseph, his two sons, and Jacob himself. Of course the 70 included only Jacob and his descendants. Acts 7:14 gives the total as 75 instead of 70 and seems to follow the Septuagint (Hebrew translation of the Old Testament), which adds a son and grandson of Manasseh and two sons and a grandson of Ephraim. In addition, there were wives (possibly 14), servants (those of Jacob's and Isaac's families) and probably some Shechemite women and children, for a total of two or three hundred persons, with all the livestock. Descendants of Abraham evidently were marrying younger and having more children. The part of the Abrahamic Covenant that promised innumerable descendants was on the way to fulfillment.

While the whole company lumbered along slowly, Jacob sent Judah (now the trusted son) ahead to learn from Joseph exactly where in Goshen they should settle. When the Hebrews arrived, Joseph came to meet Jacob in "his chariot," a special state one. "Joseph appeared before him." Because the verb used here normally applies to a divine appearance, Joseph's coming may have been especially majestic or have had the hand of God manifest in it. The meeting of Joseph and Jacob was a very emotional one, and no recorded word was expressed in their long and tearful embrace. Words could hardly do justice to the occasion anyway. Their love for each other evidently was very great. When Jacob finally did speak, he did not say, "Now let me die" (KJV), as if he wished to die, but "Now I am ready to die" (NEB). He could die at ease, knowing Joseph was all right and his family affairs were in order.

Joseph then prepared to return to Pharaoh to inform him that the Hebrews had arrived. He told his brothers that he would inform Pharaoh his family members were all shepherds and had brought their flocks and herds. And he instructed them that if Pharaoh asked them about their livelihood, they should tell him frankly they were shepherds. What Joseph sought to do was to build a case for Pharaoh's allowing the Hebrews to settle in Goshen (Joseph's earlier choice, but not yet confirmed by Pharaoh). The reason for Joseph's concern was that Egyptians considered shepherds an abomination. Settlement in Goshen would separate them from the Egyptian cattlemen of the Nile Valley and thus reduce friction with Egyptians and preserve their distinctiveness as a people. Also, if the Hebrews did not come in contact with many Egyptians, they would not intermarry with them or be greatly influenced by their idolatry. Moreover, settlement of the Hebrews in the eastern delta would make it easier for them to leave when the time came for them to return to Canaan.

Joseph's Family Before Pharaoh (47:1-12)

After Joseph's meeting with his father, he arranged an audience with Pharaoh to make formal the decision concerning settlement. First, he informed Pharaoh that his family and their flocks and herds were already in Goshen—an accomplished fact but not officially approved. Then he presented five of his brothers for a review of the situation. Presumably he chose the ones best able to handle themselves at the court and coached them on their conduct (46:33). Anticipating that Pharaoh would ask their occupation, a question commonly put to immigrants, Joseph had urged them to emphasize that they were shepherds. That they did, with the added points that they had come "to sojourn," not settle permanently, and that dire conditions in Canaan had made it necessary for them to leave. Then they requested to live in Goshen. By calling attention to an occupation detested by the Egyptians, they could expect that segregation from Egyptians on the edge of the land would be best for the Egyptians and for them. As before, Pharaoh made it clear that they were welcome to settle in Egypt: "Egypt is at your disposal." Then he reaffirmed an earlier offer to give them the best of the land (45:18) and finally got specific in permitting them to settle in Goshen. As a final evidence of goodwill, he offered to make of any of them who were especially knowledgeable supervisors of his own livestock.

Probably Joseph introduced Jacob to Pharaoh at a later time—at least the atmosphere seems to have been more informal on that occasion. "Jacob blessed Pharaoh," not just "greeted" as in some versions, but "invoked a blessing." The old man could bless a younger one, and he could experience true heartfelt gratitude to Pharaoh for his honoring of his beloved Joseph and his kindness to the rest of the family. Then Pharaoh must have been impressed with the venerable old man's age—perhaps in part because the lives of the Pharaohs generally were not extremely long. Jacob described his life as a "pilgrimage." He had enjoyed a permanent home no more than Abraham and Isaac, for he had sojourned in Mesopotamia for twenty years, then had lived in Succoth and Shechem and southern Canaan, and now was in Egypt (cf. Heb. 11:13-16, 21). His 130 years were considered "few" in comparison to the "pilgrimage" of his fathers: Abraham had lived to the age of 175 and Isaac to 180. Jacob was destined to live to 147. His years had been "difficult" too, at almost every juncture except the present one, as a review of his life would show. But better days were ahead (see comments on 47:27-28). The passage ends with a summary statement to the effect that Joseph followed up on the edict of Pharaoh and settled his relatives in Goshen and provided them with adequate food. "Land of Rameses" is a name that was applied to the region at a later time, in Moses' day or afterward.

NOTES

1. Derek Kidner, *Genesis* (Downers Grove, Ill.: Inter-Varsity, 1967, p. 205.

14

JOSEPH (3)
THE LATTER DAYS OF JOSEPH AND JACOB

GENESIS 47:13–50:26

Joseph's Economic Policy (47:13-26)

The famine created desperate conditions, especially in Canaan and Egypt (v. 13). Perhaps a much wider region was affected, but the focus of attention centered on those lands because of biblical personalities involved. The text describes the increasing plight of Egyptians and alludes to three stages in their worsening condition and the increasing grip of the crown on the whole country. First, all available money was used up to buy food, then Egyptians sold their livestock to Pharaoh, and finally they sold their land and their service to the crown according to an arrangement that required the use of one-fifth of all future crops as land rental. It is not to be assumed that one year everyone ran out of money, and the next year ran out of livestock to sell. Some would have little money and little livestock and therefore would fall into bondage sooner than others. The more wealthy could hold out longer, and some no doubt managed to ride out the famine. Individuals found themselves at different stages of economic decline. The powerful priesthoods of Egypt were able to protect their lands from crown control, and the priests received grain doles from Pharaoh's granaries. Of course those policies were not necessarily Joseph's but could have been at least partially Pharaoh's policies implemented by Joseph.

At this point it is well to ask if there is any place in Egyptian history for such major changes in the political and economic situation as Joseph's policies would have brought about. In order to deal with such a question, it is necessary to determine when Joseph may have ruled in Egypt. If one holds to the early date of the

Exodus (c. 1446) and adds 430 years for the period of Israelite sojourn in Egypt (Exodus 12:40), he will conclude that the Israelites entered Egypt about 1876. That would be early in the reign of Sesostris III (or Senwosret or Sen-Usert, 1878-1840). Sesostris was a vigorous Middle Kingdom Pharaoh who extended Egyptian control south to the second cataract and campaigned up into Syria. Also he was able to overcome the feudalistic conditions that had existed from the beginning of the Middle Kingdom (c. 2000 B.C.). He took away the power of the nobles and appointed royal officials in their stead. It is tempting to conclude that that achievement somehow was related to the famine in Joseph's day and Joseph's use of that famine to fasten royal control on all the populace of the land. Sesostris still would have been ruling when Jacob died and certainly would have permitted the burial that Genesis records.

Many would like to pull down the date of Joseph and place him during the Hyksos period. Those Asiatics began to infiltrate Egypt during the Middle Kingdom and took over the country about 1730. By that time Goshen would not have been so open to receive the Hebrews as it seems to have been in Joseph's day, and the kind of Egyptian exclusiveness that forbade Egyptians to eat with Asiatics probably had begun to break down. It is also very doubtful that the Hyksos kings ever so fully controlled the native Egyptians as Pharaoh did by the time the famine was over in Joseph's day.

Jacob's Request About His Burial (47:27-31)

Having summarized the dire privation of Egyptians during the famine, the sacred historian now alludes to contrasting conditions among the Hebrews. They amassed property and greatly increased numerically, apparently both during and after the famine. Jacob enjoyed seventeen more happy years among his increasing progeny, watching the blessing of God on the Hebrew community and basking in the glow of his son's glory as vizier of Egypt. At length, with rapidly declining faculties, he felt the end was near. Confident of the fulfillment of God's promises concerning return to the land of Canaan, Jacob extracted from Joseph a commitment to bury him with his "fathers," evidently meaning in the ancestral tomb in the cave of Machpelah at Hebron. And Israel bowed in worship and prayer.

The Blessing of Ephraim and Manasseh (48:1-22)

Within a few months of events recorded in the last chapter, Joseph received a report that his father was ill—more than the debilitating effects of old age must be meant. So Joseph decided to take his two sons, Manasseh and Ephraim, to visit the aged patriarch. It seems inconceivable that what happened was a whim of the moment on the part of Jacob. The session required a great expenditure of Jacob's strength, and his pronouncements evidently were in the plan of God. Leupold is of the conviction that Jacob and Joseph at an earlier time had discussed some such arrangement as was here made formal.[1] The writer of the book of Hebrews classified this blessing as Jacob's outstanding act of faith (Heb. 11:21), for it demonstrated his unwavering confidence in God's covenant promises.

When Jacob learned that Joseph was coming, he "pulled himself together" and "sat up on his bed" with his feet on the floor and his knees protruding from the bed. "Israel," the head of the Hebrew community and bearer of the covenant promises of God, was about to act. Clearly those covenant promises were uppermost in Israel's mind at the moment: his numerous progeny ("I will . . . make of you a company of tribes") and possession of the land of Canaan ("I will give this land to you and your seed after you as an everlasting possession"). He harked back to the marvelous appearances of God to him at Luz, ancient name of Bethel (Gen. 28:10-15; 35:6-13).

With the thought of multiplication and grouping into tribes, Jacob proceeded to the adoption of Joseph's sons as his own. They were to be adopted on a par with his two eldest sons, Reuben and Simeon, and their descendants were to enjoy full status as tribes. In fact, Reuben's birthright was given to the sons of Joseph (1 Chron. 5:1-2), and the two tribes given to Joseph probably reflect the double portion associated with the birthright. If Joseph had any additional sons, they would be attached to Ephraim or Manasseh for purposes of inheritance. Verse 7 is not an irrelevant backward glance of an old man. It provides the reason for the adoption of Joseph's sons: Joseph was a beloved son of Rachel, and Rachel died too soon—before she could bear other sons.

Then Joseph formally presented his sons to Jacob, who could not see them because he was now blind. First Israel kissed and embraced them. Then they were brought to stand between Israel's knees, a ritual action declaring them his own issue. Both of them could not stand there at the same time because they were too big—about twenty years old at the time. Next Joseph presented his sons for an official blessing, having them stand so Manasseh (the elder) was opposite Jacob's right hand and Ephraim (the younger) opposite his left. But Israel crossed his hands and recognized the second-born (with his right hand) above the firstborn (with his left). The blessing was on "Joseph," a collective noun for the two sons, referring to Joseph's double portion among the tribes. It involved a threefold invocation of God: (1) in covenant relation with the patriarchs; (2) as "Shepherd" (NIV; NEB) who had led and fed him all through life (cf. Psalm 23); (3) as "angel" in visible encounters with him and redeeming or reclaiming him in times of trouble. That great God is called on to bless the boys, to be to them all He has been in the past to Israel and his fathers. And as sons of the patriarchs may they bear the "name" of the patriarchs—have the patriarchs' character and shoulder the responsibilities that go with being in covenant relationship with God. Last, the blessing involved having many descendants so Ephraim and Manasseh could occupy and hold the promised land. Joseph was displeased to see Israel giving the chief blessing to the younger. Evidently he thought Israel had made a mistaken assumption about the order of the boys as they stood before him, so he tried to reverse his father's hands. But Israel protested that he knew what he was doing; Ephraim would be greater than Manasseh. Ephraim did possess greater numbers in the census prior to entrance into the land (Num. 1:32-35). He became the strongest tribe of all the twelve, and his name was an alternative name for the northern kingdom of Israel.

Then Jacob had a final personal word for Joseph. Jacob was about to die, but God would restore Joseph or at least his descendants to the land of Canaan. When He did, Joseph's direct lineage was to possess Shechem, which would not be subject to distribution by lot. What exactly is meant by taking that "with my sword and my bow" is debated. It cannot refer to Genesis 34, because Jacob had no part in that shameful act and condemned it; furthermore, he did not occupy the city at that time. According to Genesis 33:19, he bought a piece of land there and enjoyed peaceful relations with the inhabitants. Probably the warlike action "with my sword and my bow" refers to an event not otherwise recorded in Scripture. The tract of land was clearly identified. Joseph was buried within his own territory at the time of the conquest (Josh. 24:32), and the parcel remained distinct in Jesus' day (John 4:5).

Future of the Sons of Jacob (49:1-29)

"Then," soon after the adoption and blessing of Ephraim and Manasseh, Jacob "called for" or "summoned" all his sons for his patriarchal blessing. But what he had to say was not all pleasant; some of it involved a curse or censure. None was disinherited, however; all were sons of Abraham and destined to possess the promised land. What appears in this chapter is not just Israel's pious wish for his sons; it is an oracle, a vision for all the tribes, a prophetic blessing, a saying of destiny that describes what will happen in "days to come." The sequence of names involves first the six sons of Leah, then the four sons of the handmaids, and finally the sons of Rachel. The form of Jacob's statement is Hebrew poetic parallelism, and it should be read in a version that pays attention to literary form. Critics commonly deny that Jacob was the author of this prophetic statement, largely because they deny the supernatural and therefore predictive prophecy. Thus they try to redate predictive statements and turn them into historical accounts. But the supernatural provides the warp and woof of the Hebrew-Christian faith; without the supernatural, it is not a faith worth believing. What Israel had to say to each he said in the presence of all and provided a sobering and instructional comment for all.

Reuben (49:3-4). As firstborn, Reuben should have been characterized by dignity, power, integrity, and stability. But he was "unstable as water" (RSV) or seething as water does, characterized by unbridled license. "You shall not be foremost"; he was to be displaced from the privileges of firstborn because of fornication with Bilhah, his father's concubine (35:22). Not an outstanding personage descended from Reuben, and eventually the tribe seems to have been absorbed into the half tribe of Manasseh.

Simeon and Levi (49:5-7). Jacob scored these brothers who

joined in wicked violence at Shechem (34:25), an act from which Jacob wanted to be completely dissociated ("let me not join"). The cause of their action was their cruel and vindictive anger, and as their punishment they were to be dispersed in Israel. That indeed occurred because Simeon was largely absorbed into Judah, and Levi as the priestly tribe received forty-eight cities scattered throughout the other tribes (Josh. 21). But for one's sin one need not be condemned forever; descendants of Levi became priests and teachers of the law. And both tribes will enter the messianic Kingdom (Ezek. 44; Rev. 7:7).

Judah (49:8-12). Jacob's prophecy of Judah was particularly eloquent. True, he had sinned greatly in wrongdoing his daughter-in-law Tamar and in leading the others to sell Joseph into slavery. But he had experienced a real regeneration, as the later Joseph narrative demonstrates, and had risen to a place of respected leadership among his brothers. Judah would be prominent among the tribes of Israel ("whom your brothers will praise"), would succeed in warfare ("hand . . . on the neck of your enemies"), and would enjoy the power of empire that keeps its enemies in check (v. 10). In fact, in Judah alone royalty would reside until Messiah comes: "until he comes to whom it [the scepter] belongs" (NIV). This passage ties in directly with Ezekiel 21:26-27 (cf. Rev. 5:5). The "obedience of the nations" looks forward to the time when every knee shall bow to the universal rule of the Messiah (Isa. 45:23; Phil. 2:10-11; Rev. 5:13). Verses 11 and 12 go on to speak of conditions at the time of Christ's second coming. Commonly they are taken to refer to the abundance characteristic of His millennial reign; but there are those who refer them to judgment at His return, that is, the trampling of the winepress of His wrath[2] (Cf. Isa. 63:3; Dan. 7:9; Rev. 19:11, 14; 20:11). Of course that prophecy of kingship in Judah has in view the line of David, the Davidic Covenant promising perpetual kingship in his line (2 Sam. 7), and the eternal rule of Christ, David's greater son, on the throne of David.

Zebulun (49:13). Zebulun is the only one of the tribes in this survey that is assigned a geographical location. Although Zebulun never did obtain territory on the sea, an important caravan route from the East passed through his territory; therefore he did profit greatly from commercial activity. Probably the prophecy did not intend to allocate to Zebulun land all the way up "to Sidon" but "toward Sidon" (NIV).

Issachar (49:14-15). Whereas Zebulun would have many outside commercial contacts, Issachar would be largely restricted to domestic agricultural concerns. The people of the tribe would be diligent farmers, later occupying the territory of lower Galilee.

Dan (49:16-18). Dan ("judge") would judge his people: Samson, for instance, was from this tribe (Judg. 13:2). Verse 17 is enigmatic but may mean, "May he successfully overthrow all who wrongfully oppose him." Some consider the reference to "a serpent by the way" to refer to Dan's lack of moral commitment and tendency to encourage idolatry (Judg. 18) and therefore to be a reason why Dan was the only one of the twelve tribes omitted from Revelation 7.[3]

Gad (49:19). Gad's later decision to live in Transjordan exposed the tribe to Midianites, Ammonites, Arabians, and other marauders from the desert; but Gad would be forceful about striking back.

Asher (49:20). Jacob foresaw that Asher would settle in a fertile land that would be so productive as to provide "royal delicacies," food fit for a king—whether of Israel or some other land. As a matter of fact, Asher obtained the fruitful area along the seacoast from Carmel north to the territory of Tyre.

Naphtali (49:21). "Naphtali is a deer set free" (cf. 2 Sam. 22:34) may refer to the fleet strength of the men of Naphtali. Allotted land north of the Plain of Esdraelon, Naphtali furnished many men for the army of Barak, which was successful against the Canaanite Sisera (Judg. 4).

Joseph (49:22-26). Along with the blessing on Judah, the blessing on Joseph was abundantly rich. Joseph as a "fruitful branch" must have had in view especially the numerous descendants to come through Ephraim ("fruitful"), one of the leading tribes. The "archers" who "shot at him," enemies or persecutors (whether his brothers, Potiphar, or others), did not destroy him because "his bow remained steady." His staying power did not come from any native abilities, however, but from God. And as if to underscore how much God had been on his side, how much He had blessed, and how much He would bless, Jacob heaped up names of deity: Mighty One of Jacob, Shepherd, Rock of Israel, God of your father, the Almighty. Power, tender loving care, and covenant commitment are among concepts involved in those ascriptions. Then Jacob heaped blessing on top of blessing: "of heaven" (rainfall); "of the deep" (subterranean waters); and "of breasts and womb" (reproduction among men and livestock).

Benjamin (49:27). The portrayal of Benjamin as a ravenous wolf seems to portray aggressive activity, warlike character. And "prey to devour and plunder to divide" indicate the tribe's general success. The Benjamites were farmers and archers and slingers (Judg. 20:16; 2 Chron. 14:8). The judge Ehud (Judg. 3:15), Saul (1 Sam. 9:1) and Jonathan, and the apostle Paul (Rom. 11:1) were Benjamites.

Jacob's Death and Burial (49:28—50:13)

Jacob's prophetic blessing had been one of his finest acts, and it had required almost all his remaining available strength. Aware that he was about to die, he gave instructions for his burial in the cave of Machpelah; he had already won Joseph's promise to bury him in Canaan (Gen. 47:30). At this point the first reference is made to the earlier death of Leah, whom Jacob had buried in the cave of Machpelah. (She had not entered Egypt with the clan.) Finished with his instructions, Jacob breathed his last and died at the age of 147 (Gen. 47:28).

No doubt all the sons of Jacob were present at his death, but Joseph's grief is especially mentioned because of his closeness to his father and his promise to care for him at death. Promptly Joseph directed the physicians in his service to embalm Jacob. Hebrews did not embalm but normally buried the deceased the same day; Egyptians embalmed at least upper-class persons. And of course embalming was necessary in this case if the body was to be taken on a long trip to Canaan. Why Joseph had physicians instead of the embalmers embalm his father is uncertain. Physicians were equally capable of performing the task and perhaps they would have employed less of the pagan religious ritual than members of the embalmers' guild would have. The text observes that the embalming process took forty days and the mourning process seventy days, the former being included in the latter period. Actually the time spent on embalming varied from person to person and from time to time. A seventy-day mourning period is just short of the normal seventy-two-day mourning for a Pharaoh. Although the mummification process differed from period to period and person to person, several generalizations may be made. First, an incision was made in the left side and the liver, lungs, stomach, and intestines were removed and treated separately. Ultimately these were placed in four stone containers known as canopic jars, which were sealed and had their lids carved to represent human heads during the Middle Kingdom. In Joseph's day the brain normally was left in place. Second, the body was dried out over an extended period of time by continued application of natron, a mixture of sodium carbonate and sodium bicarbonate. Third, the body was washed with a natron bath and anointed with cedar oil and other ointments. Fourth, the chest and abdominal cavities were stuffed with linen soaked in resin. Fifth, the body was wrapped with endless yards of linen strips soaked in resin, and often resin was poured over the mummy when it was partially wrapped. Finally, the body was placed in a painted wooden coffin inscribed with religious formulae.

When the seventy days were over, Joseph appealed to Pharaoh for permission to bury his father in the tomb he had "hewed out" for himself in Canaan. That request was channeled through officials of the court (v. 4) instead of in person because presumably Joseph still wore mourning clothes and could not appear before Pharaoh in them. He would wear such clothing until the burial occurred. In sending the request, he made it clear he had sworn an oath to his father to bury him there. Pharaoh gave his permission for Joseph to go; and so great were Joseph's position and reputation in Egypt that many officials of the court and other dignitaries went along. The company included, besides those government leaders, Joseph's family, his brothers and their wives, chariot drivers, servants to provide eating and sleeping facilities for the company, and soldiers. Well over a hundred persons, with chariots and wagons to carry tents, food and other supplies, composed the caravan. Presumably Joseph was still vizier of Egypt, even though the famine was well behind him. Whether or not any of Joseph's brothers were then in the employ of Pharaoh is not known. If Pharaoh had any initial worry about the return of the Hebrews, it was eliminated by the fact that they left their children and possessions behind in Egypt.

The company was gone for a long time. They probably took a circuitous route around the south end of the Dead Sea and then north through Edom and Moab. At a place called Abel Mizraim, east of the Jordan, they held a solemn ceremony of mourning for seven days and then proceeded to Mamre and the cave of Machpelah to bury Jacob. Then they all returned to Egypt. The entire patriarchal family had seen the promised land once more and had been reminded that God had promised it to them and their descendants forever. But all was not yet ready for their settlement there.

Joseph's Last Days (50:14-26)

With Jacob gone, Joseph's brothers feared that Joseph might punish them for their earlier treatment of him. In fact, they were so apprehensive that they did not dare go in person or send one of their number to seek his favor. Rather, they sent a messenger to him. They reported that, before he died, Jacob had issued a commandment that Joseph should forgive his brothers for their sins against him. They requested therefore that he truly forgive them. If Jacob did actually intervene on behalf of the ten, he demonstrated some lack of certainty concerning Joseph's intentions. But perhaps the brothers merely contrived that statement to protect themselves. In either case there would be a reflection on the genuineness of Joseph's earlier forgiveness and a mistrust of him that would be enough to cause him to weep. Either because he delayed to reply to them or because they really intended the message sent as an ice breaker, the brothers then came to him and prostrated themselves before him as they had when they knew him only as the vizier of Egypt. Shades of Joseph's first dream!

Joseph's response was, "Fear not. Am I in the place of God?" It was God's prerogative to judge men for their sins, not his. Then he repeated in essence his earlier statement to them that though they intended evil, God in His sovereign purposes meant it for good to the end that He might do "what is now being done," or "as has actually happened"—the keeping alive of a great multitude. The multitude included not only the entire Hebrew clan but also other peoples of Canaan and the entire nation of Egypt. Joseph took the larger view; what happened to him was not nearly so important as the greater good that came out of it. "I will provide for you" did not now refer to a dole from the public granaries, because the famine was over, but rather the protection and watch-care that he could provide by his influential position at court.

Between verses 21 and 22 more than fifty years passed. Joseph was no longer vizier of Egypt and the Pharaoh under which he had served had long since passed away. Joseph had lived long enough to begin to see fulfillment of Jacob's blessing of "breast and womb" (49:25); he saw the third generation of Ephraim's children. Having reached the age of 110, Joseph realized he was about to die. Then he recalled to his brothers that God "on oath" had promised the land of Canaan to Abraham, Isaac, and Jacob and their descendants. Some day God would take the Hebrews back there. And he made them swear "on oath" that they would then carry his bones with them to the promised land. So when he died they embalmed him and placed him in a coffin, ready for the removal—a witness to the future emigration to the land of promise.

So ends the book of Genesis, which may be thought of as a book of beginnings or a book of the doings of early mankind—seen both in great wickedness and great faith. But it is preeminently a saga of the acts of a sovereign, majestic, and holy God as He brought into being the heavens and the earth (and equipped them), mankind, and ultimately the Hebrew people—through whom He would send the Messiah to bring redemption and some day to reign as sovereign Lord over a world at peace.

NOTES

1. H. C. Leupold, *Exposition of Genesis*, 2 vols. (Grand Rapids: Baker, 1942), 2:1145.
2. Harold G. Stigers, *A Commentary on Genesis* (Grand Rapids: Zondervan, 1976), p. 328.
3. John J. Davis, *Paradise to Prison* (Grand Rapids: Baker, 1975), p. 300.

BIBLIOGRAPHY

Archer, Gleason L., Jr. *A Survey of Old Testament Introduction.* Rev. ed. Chicago: Moody, 1974.

Atkinson, Basil. *The Book of Genesis.* Chicago: Moody, 1957.

Barnhouse, Donald G. *Genesis.* Grand Rapids: Zondervan, 1973.

Calvin, John. *Commentaries on the First Book of Moses Called Genesis.* 2 vols. Grand Rapids: Eerdmans, 1948.

Carroll, B. H. *Studies in Genesis.* Nashville: Broadman, 1937.

Davis, John J. *Paradise to Prison.* Grand Rapids: Baker, 1975.

Dods, Marcus. *The Book of Genesis.* Edinburgh: T. & T. Clark, n.d.

Frair, Wayne, and Davis, P. William. *The Case for Creation.* Rev. ed. Chicago: Moody, 1972.

Hughes, Albert. *A Supplanter Becomes a Prince.* Toronto: Evangelical Publishers, 1934.

Jamieson, Robert. "Genesis," in *A Commentary on the Old and New Testaments.* Vol 1. Grand Rapids: Eerdmans, 1945.

Keil, C. F. and Delitzsch, Franz, eds. *Biblical Commentary on the Old Testament.* Vol 1. Grand Rapids: Eerdmans, n.d.

Kevan, E. F. "Genesis" in *The New Bible Commentary.* Edited by F. Davidson, A. M. Stibbs, and E. F. Kevan. Grand Rapids: Eerdmans, 1953.

Kidner, Derek. *Genesis.* Downers Grove, Ill.: Inter-Varsity, 1967.

Lange, John P. "Genesis," in *A Commentary on the Holy Scriptures.* New York: Scribner's, 1915.

Leupold, H. C. *Exposition of Genesis.* 2 vols. Grand Rapids: Baker, 1942.

Luther, Martin. *Luther's Commentary on Genesis.* Translated by J. Theodore Mueller. 2 vols. Grand Rapids: Zondervan, 1958.

Morris, Henry M. *The Genesis Record.* Grand Rapids: Baker, 1976.

Newman, Robert C. and Eckelmann, Herman J., Jr., *Genesis One and the Origin of the Earth.* Downers Grove, Ill.: Inter-Varsity, 1977.

Parrot, André. *Abraham and His Times.* Philadelphia: Fortress, 1962.

Stigers, Harold G. *A Commentary on Genesis.* Grand Rapids: Zondervan, 1976.

Unger, Merrill F. *Archeology and the Old Testament*. Grand Rapids: Zondervan, 1954.

————. *Introductory Guide to the Old Testament*. Grand Rapids: Zondervan, 1951.

Van Haitsma, John P. *The Supplanter Undeceived*. Grand Rapids: Van Haitsma, 1941.

Wood, Leon J. *Genesis*. Grand Rapids: Zondervan, 1975.

Yates, Kyle M., Sr. "Genesis," in *The Wycliffe Bible Commentary*. Edited by Charles F. Pfeiffer and Everett F. Harrison. Chicago: Moody, 1962.

Young, Davis A. *Creation and Flood*. Grand Rapids: Baker, 1977.

Young, Edward J. *Studies in Genesis One*. Philadelphia: Presbyterian and Reformed, 1964.

Youngblood, Ronald. *Faith of Our Fathers (Genesis 12-50)*. Glendale, Calif.: Gospel Light/Regal, 1976.

————. *How It All Began (Genesis 1-11)*. Glendale, Calif.: Gospel Light/Regal, 1980.